Return to
Gill Park

Return to Gill Park

by AMY GORDON

Holiday House / New York

With many thanks to the students who helped
create *The String Man*: Jack Borland,
Naomi Braude, James Casale, Parker Cohn,
Katherine Frank, Eun Lee, Rahim Manji,
Hyun Jin Park, Kate Pistel, Chloe Reid, and
Charlotte Turner.

And many thanks to Jutta Mason,
the "Mitch Bloom" of Dufferin Grove Park
in Toronto, Canada.

Mr. Kim's knowledge of the alphabet comes
from the *Oxford Family Encyclopedia,*
George Philip Limited,
Oxford University Press, 1997.

Library of Congress Cataloging-in-Publication Data

Gordon, Amy, 1949–
    Return to Gill Park / by Amy Gordon.—1st ed.
        p.   cm.
    Summary: When thirteen-year-old Willy Wilson returns to Gloria to
enroll in Gill Park Gallery School, he finds himself in the middle of a
politically backed struggle to save the park and to solve a treasure hunt.
    ISBN-10: 0-8234-1998-3 (hardcover)
    ISBN-13: 978-0-8234-1998-2
    [1. Parks—Fiction.   2. Friendship—Fiction.   3. Schools—Fiction.
4. Art—Fiction.]   I. Title.

PZ7.G65Ret   2006
[Fic]—dc22   2005050335

For Jane and George

one

I love coming into my living room and seeing
a clean, white, vacuumed carpet.
—*Marcia Wilson*

My midterm report card had a definite theme.

Ms. Goat said I wasn't following through on homework assignments. Mrs. Polar Bear said my work
was sloppy. Mr. Giraffe said I did not study ade-
quately for tests. Mr. Kangaroo said I did not initiate
enough in the classroom, and Ms. Nervous Little
Bird said I needed to ask more questions and also
that I wasn't writing down the correct assignments.

All this made my mother's shoulders droopy and
her face tight. My father started pacing again, a
habit I thought he had given up. Even our goldfish

seemed a bit panicky, swimming in circles even more than usual.

"Willy, how could you have had the determination to find Otto Pettingill last summer when he disappeared, but you can't even finish a homework assignment?" Dad asked.

"I'm different when I'm at Gill Park," I said. "Can't we move to Gloria?"

But instantly I regretted the suggestion. I'd stayed with my aunt Bridget in her apartment by the park all last summer, and when the owner of the park, Otto Pettingill, mysteriously disappeared, I found him. I also found out that his lawyer tried to sell the park right out from under his nose. Mr. P. and I had become friends after that. He taught me how to read music and how to play the violin, and then when he died at the end of the summer, he left the park to me in his will.

No, I didn't want my parents living in Gloria— Gill Park was my world, not theirs.

"You spend too much time on the computer," my father said. "We're going to have to take it away from you."

"I'm on the computer because I need to be able to keep in touch with Gill Park," I said. I felt like shouting, but I didn't. "Gareth and Aunt Bridget keep me informed. I'm the owner of Gill Park. It's my job."

"Your job is your schoolwork," my mother said grimly.

But they didn't say anything more about taking

away the computer. That was a good thing because that night Gareth sent a terrible message.

"Willy! This gang of kids attacked the park. They started spraying everything in sight with blue spray paint—the statue and the fountain and the benches and the trees. What a mess! They were wearing blue masks and had blue paint all over them so no one could tell who they were. Dad and Mitch Bloom are looking into it, but you need to come out here."

"I have to go to Gloria this weekend," I told my parents the next day.

My mother said, "You can't. You've got that history research paper. And that fund-raiser car wash on Saturday morning, and a soccer game on Saturday afternoon."

I groaned. My mother knew my schedule a lot better than I did.

Then the school's assistant headmaster called and told my mother he thought she and Dad should come in for a meeting to talk about me. When they came home, Mom's face was even more pinched. "They think you have ADD," said Mom.

"ADD?" My heart sank.

"Attention deficit disorder," said Mom, as if I didn't know. A lot of kids in my school had ADD.

Dad was furious. "It's ridiculous," he kept saying. "He does not have ADD. They're just not teaching him properly at that school. All that money we're

paying, and the best they can come up with is ADD."
He started pacing and pulling his hair.

"They don't know for sure, of course," Mom said.
"That's why they're recommending testing, but per-
sonally, I think he just needs to bond more with kids
in his class." She suddenly seemed to notice I was
sitting on the couch right next to her. "How about
inviting some of your classmates over, Willy? You
made friends this summer, so we know you can. That
Kyle McNulty seems a bit like Gareth, and then there's
that nice-looking Cody Harris. I see his mother at
the Y all the time. I could ask her to get Cody to invite
you over."

"Mom. I'm thirteen years old. I don't need you to
arrange playdates for me."

"Maybe having you take up the violin wasn't such
a good idea," said Dad. "I mean, it seems unhealthy
for a thirteen-year-old boy to be in his room all night
practicing the violin."

I looked at my parents. They both looked so worried. Then I remembered how at the end of the summer I had promised myself I would make Mom laugh
once a day. I wasn't doing very well. I wasn't sure I
had even made her laugh once a month. "How about
I hang out at the mall every afternoon, Mom. Would
you feel better about me then?"

My mother didn't even crack a smile. I'd have to
work on the humor.

The day before the test for ADD, Dad came home
and said, "Marcia, Willy—there's something I'd like
to discuss with you." He looked serious, and he made

us come into the living room and sit down. He paced around the room, jingling the coins in his pockets. He seemed to be having a hard time getting started.

"Please, Bill, get on with it," my mother said. "You're making me anxious."

"Well, it's a bit of a coincidence, really, but my sister called me today just to check on Willy. So I filled Bridget in on what's been happening, and she came up with quite an idea." He stopped pacing. I sat on the edge of my seat. "She suggested Willy go to the school that young scamp Liesl is going to. You know, the school that Mr. Pettingill left Belle Vera in charge of."

I could feel myself beginning to fill up like a balloon expanding with helium. I might get to go to school with Liesl Summer!

Liesl was the most unusual kid I'd ever known, probably because she was an orphan, and Mr. Pettingill, who had had some pretty definite ideas about how kids should be raised, had been her guardian. For one thing, Mr. P. had never allowed her to go to school. For another, even though she lived with a really nice French lady named Belle Vera, she had always been able to wear and do exactly whatever she liked. Mostly she liked wearing weird, ragtag clothes and hanging out in the park drawing. And let me tell you, that kid could draw, better than Leonardo da Vinci, or someone like that.

Mr. P. changed his mind about Liesl going to school. He thought he'd made a mistake, and then finally, he let her go live with Mitch Bloom, the old man who sold flowers in the park and lived in a tree house and understood Liesl better than anyone else.

Liesl was a wild little kid, all right, with a temper that made me shake in my shoes sometimes, but by the end of the summer, we had ended up becoming friends. I liked the idea of going to school with her.

"The school's in an art gallery," Dad was saying, "and it's designed to help kids who are having trouble in regular schools. Bridget says there's a young man teaching there who's very tough, so it's not that it's easier than regular school—"

"But where would he live?"

Dad swallowed hard. "With my sister," he said.

"You want Willy to go live with *Bridget*?" Mom raised her voice. She looked at Dad as if he'd grown furry ears or another nose. "All you've ever done all your life is complain about her—how she's flighty and irresponsible and doesn't live in reality."

"I know, I know," said Dad, beginning to pace again. "We haven't always seen eye to eye, but this past summer . . . Well, I see her differently. She's had to manage on her own since Roger died, and she does quite amazingly, and honestly, she's good with Willy. And think about it, Marcia. Willy has more friends there than he does here, and he'll be near the park—"

Mom threw up her arms. "What was Otto Pettingill thinking, putting that kind of responsibility on a young boy? And what about high school, Bill? Where will he go to high school?"

"Well, the school might continue all the way through high school," Dad said lamely.

Mom rolled her eyes. "Is it even accredited? It's in an *art* gallery, Bill! How is he ever going to get into college?"

My father stopped pacing and came over and sat down on the couch beside Mom. He took her hand in his. "I worry about those kinds of things, too, Marcia. But let's just take one day at a time. Willy is having trouble in school right now. This just seems like a practical solution to his problems."

"And it's also . . . it's also that he's growing up so fast," said Mom, looking at me for the first time. Her eyes were filling up with tears, and she was making me feel pretty choked up, too. "Once he's there, he'll never want to come home. I'll miss his growing up."

"He won't be so far away, Marcia," said Dad. "We can see him all the time."

Mom started crying for real. "But . . . we won't . . . he won't . . . he likes your sister more than me."

"Oh, Mom." I got down on my hands and knees and started whimpering like a dog. I bounded over to her and rested my head on her knees.

"Oh, Willy," she said, half laughing, half crying.

A picture flashed inside my head. I was sitting at the table in Aunt Bridget's kitchen doing my homework while Aunt Bridget was in the living room making costumes. That's what she did for a living. I wasn't having any trouble at all concentrating, because I was living right across the street from Gill Park.

two

Everything is interesting to me.

—JinYoung Kim

I was sadder than I thought I would be, leaving my old school. After all, I had been there all my life. It was all worn-in and familiar, like an old pair of sneakers. The kids in my class gave me a going-away party. Kyle and Cody acted as if I had been their best buddy. Some of the girls even cried.

The school people gave us a hard time. They said we were walking away from a good education and that I was going to fall even further behind at this weird school I was going to. I kept waking up in the middle of the night wondering if it was all a big mistake.

But then I'd start thinking about how great it was going to be to see Gareth and Liesl all the time instead of Cody and Kyle.

The next Saturday morning, Dad and Mom and I drove to Gloria together. Dad wanted us to meet with Belle Vera and JinYoung Kim, the young teacher who taught with Belle at the Gill Park Gallery School.

The trip seemed to take forever. The two-and-a-half-hour ride felt like ten hours. It didn't help that Mom cried on and off the whole time. When we finally got off the highway and turned into the narrow streets of Gloria, my heart lifted. Gloria was a real city, with tall buildings and tons of people and cars and something to look at everywhere you turned—the opposite of my boring little town.

There was a lot of traffic. Dad had to drive slowly. "It's going to take us an hour to go one block," he complained. "It'd be faster to walk."

I didn't mind crawling along. I was so happy to be back in Gloria. Sometimes when you go away to a place, it fits you better than the place you came from. Or maybe when you go to a new place, you can sort of molt and get a new skin so people look at you differently.

That's what had happened to me at Gill Park last summer.

No one had ever laughed at my jokes before, but Aunt Bridget thought I was funny. I'd been lousy at sports at home, but Gareth Pugh, the coach of the Gorilla baseball team, needed me to play first base, and I did fine. There wasn't really anyone at home I'd call a buddy, but now both Gareth and Liesl were my best friends. I'd gone along all my life being boring Willy Wilson, and now Mitch Bloom and Belle Vera treated me like I was a hero. And most of all, Mr. Pettingill had believed I could be the owner of his park.

Looking out the window now, I just soaked in everything about Gloria, and best of all, just up ahead on the right was the park.

The iron railing that went all around it had a fresh coat of black paint. It was classy looking, all right. If that gang came along and messed it up with their spray paint, it would make me really mad.

And then we saw them—as if just thinking about them had made them appear—a swarm of kids dressed in blue. Their hair was slicked up into blue spikes, and they'd covered their eyes with blue masks. They were darting in and out of the slowly moving traffic. Then I realized that one of them moved in a way that was familiar to me.

My heart jolted. It didn't matter that the kid was wearing a mask. I recognized the rattiness of that pointed face.

"Hey!" I yelled. "That's *Dillon*!"

"What?"

"That kid who just ran by, he's Dillon Deronda, the pitcher for the Sharks. You know, the team we played at the end of the summer when you came and watched."

"That boy who was so unbelievably good?" Dad asked.

"Yeah, I'm sure of it."

We saw a stream of kids racing now, in between the cars, yelling, whooping, leaping.

"Good grief," said Mom. "Where are the police in this town?"

She and Dad muttered about the Blue Gang all the way to the Gill Park Gallery School.

The school was on the east side of town, right across from the park.

"It's a lovely building," Mom admitted as we stood outside for a moment, taking it in. Tall trees grew out front, their branches growing straight up, looking like the arms of basketball players reaching for a ball. The building itself was four stories with tall, narrow windows. Stone flowers and leaves and chipmunks and squirrels and birds were carved all over it.

"This doesn't really feel like a school," Mom said as we walked in.

I couldn't help agreeing with her. After coming through the front door, we were standing in a lobby that had been turned into a museum store. There were carousels with postcards on them and tables stacked with glossy art books. Set back a bit was a counter, the cost of going to the gallery posted above it.

A woman with spiky red hair and neon green eyes sat behind the counter. She was wearing a black T-shirt with a yellow rhinoceros on it. "Good morning," she said brightly. "Are you coming to see the Dowling Exhibit or just the regular gallery?"

"Actually, my son will be going to school here," Dad said.

"Ooh, that's fantastic," she said, her green eyes lighting up even more. She came out from behind the counter. Besides the rhinoceros T-shirt, she was wearing a blue plaid skirt and knee-high yellow boots. She put out a hand. "You must be Willy Wilson." She squeezed my hand hard. "We are happy to have a hero for a new student." She turned to shake my parents' hands. "I am Itsuko Furukawa," she said. "I am curator of the museum and also the art history teacher of the Gill Park Gallery School."

"How do you do?" Mom said stiffly. I could see she was having a hard time. Itsuko Furukawa did not look like any teacher we had ever seen.

"Belle Vera and JinYoung Kim are upstairs in the main classroom waiting for you. Just head up the stairs." She pointed behind her.

We walked across a floor made of black and white marble squares, passing a giant mirror, with a huge vase filled with dried flowers in front of it. Marble statues stood between marble columns. Some of the statues weren't wearing much. I glanced at Mom to see how she might be taking this.

"Imagine going to school in a place like this every day," Mom said, shaking her head. I couldn't tell if she thought that was a good or a bad thing.

"I'm sure you could come here, too, Mom," I said. "They probably take people of all ages here."

"Silly!" Mom laughed, and I couldn't help smiling. Gill Park was working its magic. I was funnier here than I was at home, and Mom finally looked less crumpled up. She wasn't even crying anymore.

We went up white marble steps that curved up and around and around, with a brass banister that felt good under my hand. The stairs were low, easy to climb. I could see the park framed in the windows, a slightly different view each time we spiraled up. I felt a beat of happiness. Every day I came to school, I'd see my park.

At the top of the stairs, we were greeted by a big, burly guy in a guard's uniform. He tipped his hat and said, "Good morning." His face was very white, and he had large, dark eyes.

"We're looking for Belle Vera," Dad said.

"That-a-way," said the guard, pointing.

We kept going through a short hallway and walked into a room mostly taken up by a long wooden table, where Belle Vera and JinYoung Kim were sitting.

"Vill-ee!" Belle pushed back her chair and oomphed up and out of it. She came right over and wrapped her arms around me and hugged me hard. "I have been so desolated not to see you. Why have you delayed so in your visit to us?"

She made me feel as if it had been a hundred years since she had last seen me, instead of only two months. I realized how much I liked her plumpness and rosy cheeks and all the laugh lines around her eyes.

"And voilà, our *professeur,* Monsieur JinYoung Kim."

JinYoung Kim stood up, too. He was only slightly taller than I was. His head was sunk down into a blue button-down shirt, which was tucked into a pair of khaki pants. He was wearing a dark blue tie. He actually looked a lot like the teachers back at my old school. I didn't know what I was expecting, but not someone who looked so teacherish.

His head poked up out of his shirt, and he bobbed it at us. "I am honored to meet you," he said.

"Please seat yourselves," said Belle. "We shall tell you some things about our school."

Everyone sat down. Mom perched on the edge of her chair and nervously kept smoothing the knees of her red-and-black-plaid slacks. Dad took a pen out of his jacket pocket and a pad of yellow legal paper out of his briefcase.

"My job," said Belle, "is to teach Liesl to read and to write—imagine, to be at her age learning this for the first time. But she is a very bright, eager pupil. I teach also my own beautiful language, *le français,* but you may choose any language to learn, Vill-ee, and we shall find you a teacher. And JinYoung," she added, nodding at him, "he teaches most everything else."

"And William, you will kindly call me Mister Kim," he said, turning to me. "Because I am young and you are young, we need the *mister* in between us. I will be your teacher, not your friend."

Mom was smiling now, looking pleased.

Dad cleared his throat. "Tell us about yourself, Mr. Kim. What are your qualifications?"

Mr. Kim spoke right up, leaning forward and straightening his tie. "As an undergraduate, I majored in physics and languages. Now I am a graduate student majoring in education at the University of Gloria. My father, he would like me to be a doctor, but I tell him I like nothing more than to talk and to teach." He bobbed his head and grinned for the first time. "When my father is disappointed, I tell him it is all his fault. You see, when he first came to this country from Korea, he got a job helping a man who made hot-air balloons. He hardly had a dime to his name. Now he owns the balloon company, and he has put all his five children through college." Mr. Kim cocked his head to one side. "Growing up with all those balloons, I just got filled up with a lot of hot air! I can't help wanting to talk and to teach."

Dad laughed politely, but Mom leaned forward. "Do you think you can teach my son? He has trouble in school. They say he has attention issues."

Mr. Kim looked fully at me. I felt myself turn red. "William is not a car," he said finally. "I cannot look under the hood and say, 'This is a good car.' I cannot take him out for a test-drive. All I can say is, if William wants to learn, he will learn. Do you want to learn, William?" he asked.

"Uh," I stuttered. "I . . . I . . ."

"Oh yes, *I*," Mr. Kim jumped in. "*I* is the ninth letter of the alphabet, and it comes from the Semitic letter yod, meaning 'hand.' In Spanish the pronoun *I* is *yo*. The Greeks called it iota." We all looked at him in silence. "You see, I told you. I am full of hot air!"

By shifting in my seat, I could see through to the hall. The big, burly guard was standing just outside the doorway, peering in at us and listening. He caught my eye and winked. I found myself smiling back at him.

"So, William, I will see you Monday morning. On time," said Mr. Kim, standing. "An honor to meet you," he said again, his head poking up out of his collar. He bobbed at Mom, Dad, and then at me before marching out of the room.

"So, voilà," said Belle, also standing. "As you see, our Mr. Kim knows every little thing." She patted me on the shoulder. "And now I, too, am on my way. I go to the park to see the progress of the oven."

I nodded, knowing that Mitch and Belle were working together on building a community bake oven for the park and a skating rink and a warming hut to go along with it. Now she kissed me on both cheeks and oomphed her way out of the room. It was a relief knowing that she, at least, would be there on Monday along with Mr. Kim.

"Well, Willy," Mom said as we climbed into the car, "what an adventure!"

She babbled on to Dad about how great the Gill Park Gallery School was going to be. I looked out the window at the school and wondered if I was going to like being taught by someone who knew every-thing.

three

All the sounds in my apartment keep me
company—the squeak of the water faucets,
the creak on the stairs,
the gurgle of the coffeemaker,
the scraping of the bedroom door on the floor.
—*Bridget McTaggart*

When we opened the door to Aunt Bridget's apartment, Gareth Pugh and Liesl Summer were there,
standing in her living room, which was just as cluttered as I remembered. Piles of fabric were heaped
beside a sewing machine on her worktable. And
over in the corner, I was happy to see the dress-
maker's form that Uncle Roger had named Flora,

and curled up beside her on the floor, Sophie, Aunt Bridget's cat.

First, Aunt Bridget gave me a huge hug, and then, Gareth flung himself at me, thumping me hard on the back. It had only been two months since I'd seen him, but he seemed taller.

"Hey, Willy, it's so great you're coming to live here. We can keep your baseball skills going all winter. And hey, look, my braces are gone. What do you think?" He grinned, showing every tooth in his head.

"Can't look straight at him," said Aunt Bridget. "You'll be blinded by his beauty."

"He does look a little different," I admitted.

"But he still has hat hair," Aunt Bridget teased. Gareth wore a baseball cap all the time, so that he had a permanent dent all around his head.

Liesl was the real shocker, though. When I had first met her, she had worn this horrible cap that was the color of someone's infected tonsils, with long, snarly hair poking out from under it. By the end of the summer, she'd had a haircut and was wearing more normal kid clothes, like T-shirts and shorts. Now her hair was longish again, but combed. She had on a tight T-shirt, tight pants, earrings all up and down her earlobes, and rings on eight out of ten fingers. What really got to me was what she had on her feet. Usually she wore a pair of holey red sneakers. Now she had on sandals, and her toenails were painted bright red.

"Hey, Willy, I hear you're going to my school.

That is totally cool. You are really, really going to like it. Mr. JinYoung Kim is the best."

Gareth grinned as he saw me staring at Liesl. "Don't mind her," he said. "This is one of Liesl's cool days. She has the teenage look going, even though she's not even a teenager yet. But tomorrow she'll look more like the Liesl we all know and love."

"Mitch Bloom says I can reinvent myself," said Liesl, tossing her head. "He says I can be anything I want. So I'm going to be cool on Mondays, Fridays, and Saturdays and geeky on Tuesdays, Wednesdays, and Thursdays."

"And on Sundays you'll want to relax," said Aunt Bridget. "Unless you want to be in a play. My good friend Jack Mack is starting up a theater for kids in the new Art Factory—where you're painting that mural, Liesl—and he's counting on kids being able to rehearse on Sunday afternoons."

Liesl nodded. Looking at her long fingers, I was reminded of what a good artist she was, and I remembered now that Gareth had told me she'd actually been hired to do a huge painting in an old factory that was being converted into studios.

"Is Jack Mack related to Zack Mack?" I asked. "The guy who played shortstop for the Sharks and also played the harmonica?"

Aunt Bridget nodded. "He's Zack's dad," she said. "Jack and I went to college together and acted in a lot of plays, and when we got out, we started our own theater company. It sure was fun for a few years." She smiled, tucking some loose strands of her curly hair behind her ears. "Then I got married, and Jack got married, and I started making costumes, and he started writing plays. Then my Roger died, and his Angela died, and well, we ran into each other a few months ago and we've been going out." Aunt Bridget blushed a little, but I could see she was happy talking about Jack Mack. "And now he's asked me to codirect his new company and make costumes. And what's really exciting is that he's written an original play called *The String Man,* and pretty soon he'll be looking for kids to try out for it."

My heart leaped a little. I'd always wanted to be in a play, but Mom never let me sign up for the ones at school, because she thought I wouldn't have enough time to do my homework.

"I might be interested in a small part," I said, trying not to sound too enthusiastic while Mom was standing right there.

"If I'm in the play, I'll want a big part," said Gareth.

"I'm going to go check in with your dad," my father said to him. "There are some unsettled things about Mr. Pettingill's estate he wants to go over with me."

My throat felt achy, the way it did every time I thought about Mr. P. dying. I hadn't known him very long, but he was the first older person ever to take a real interest in me, and the first one not to be disappointed in me in some way. And it went the other way, too. He was the first grown-up I was ever really curious about. He was so different from anyone I'd ever known. He had such strong opinions about everything—about how kids should be raised, about how you went about learning things, about how people would be happier if they listened to music all the time.

He had this setup in his apartment where he played every kind of instrument, and his music came into the park through speakers. All day long you'd hear the music, and it sort of wove through everything you did—whether you were walking along or watching Liesl draw or playing baseball.

"Whatever happened to that Roland Brookings creep?" Liesl asked as Dad went out the door with his briefcase. Roland Brookings, Jr., had been Mr. P.'s lawyer, the one who had tried to sell the park behind Mr. P.'s back. When Mr. P. found out, he fired him and hired Gareth's dad in his place.

"No one really knows," said Aunt Bridget thoughtfully. "Mr. P. never pressed any sort of charges. Brookings was just left to stew in his disappointment at not getting his hands on the most prime real estate in the city of Gloria—he and his buddy Frank Featherstone," she added with a shudder. "Who is, by the way, on the cover of last Sunday's *Gloria Times Magazine*." She poked through a pile of papers on a table by the couch. "Here it is. I guess he's being featured because he's putting up all these new apartment buildings in the South Park."

I couldn't help taking a good look at the photograph of Frank Featherstone. I had never seen him face-to-face, only caught a glimpse of him in Roland

Brooking's office when I had hidden behind the chair he was sitting in. All I'd been able to see were his fancy loafers and the golfers on the cuff buttons of his blazer.

I didn't much like what I saw now. He had a big, fleshy, flabby face, with a sort of wormy smile, and even his eyebrows seemed to say "Aren't I great?"

"I don't think I'm going to keep Frank up on my refrigerator," Aunt Bridget said, wrinkling her nose.

Mom wanted to talk to Aunt Bridget about how to take care of me—what I should eat, when I should do my homework, how I should do my homework, when I should go to bed, when I should practice the violin, how I should brush my teeth—so she and Aunt Bridget went into the kitchen to talk.

Gareth flopped himself down on Aunt Bridget's couch. I sat next to him, and Liesl sat cross-legged on the floor.

"Hey, I saw Dillon Deronda in that Blue Gang getup on our way in today," I said, remembering suddenly.

"Wow," Gareth said, pulling off his cap and rubbing his hands through his hair. "Maybe he's getting revenge on the park because the Gorillas beat his team."

"That was over two months ago," I said. "No one takes baseball that seriously." I gave Gareth a friendly punch. "Even you," I said.

"I wonder if Zack Mack is part of the Blue Gang," he said. "I mean, he *was* one of the Sharks."

"Aw, Zack Mack wouldn't hurt a flea," said Liesl.

"Besides, he goes to my school, and I'd know if he was doing something like that."

My school now, too, I thought.

"Look, I'm going to the park right now," I said, jumping up. "I want to see it. And I want to tell Mitch about Dillon."

We told Mom and Aunt Bridget where we were going, and then Gareth, Liesl, and I took off, racing down the old, creaking, wooden steps of Aunt Bridget's apartment building. We ran across the street and through the gates into the park. *Zap, zap, zap.* As soon as we stepped inside, I could feel energy zinging like electricity through my veins. I leaped and opened my arms wide, filling my lungs with Gill Park air.

Someone was in Mr. Pettingill's apartment playing music. After he died, people took turns going there, signing up for times to play instruments or to sing. Now someone was playing something fancy on the piano—chords were all piling up on each other like the cumulus clouds in my science book.

Gill Park was one perfect place to be.

four

I like the idea that trees can grow taller
than any other living thing, but they
can also exist in miniature.

—*Mitch Bloom*

As we approached the statue of Colonel Pettingill on
his horse I stopped for a moment. His sword was
still held high and the plaque still explained he had
ridden with Theodore Roosevelt. But now he was
covered with blue spray paint.

"I don't get it," I said. "Doesn't Dillon spend most
of his life hanging out in the park? He'd be nothing
without the baseball field."

Before Gareth could answer, a tall girl came running over to us. "Leese. Hey, Leese!" she called, her dark face and eyes glowing as she approached Liesl. "Good evening, Leese."

"Oh hi, Kizzi," said Liesl in a bored sort of way.

"It's Saturday, so you're still being cool today, I see," she said. She smiled a huge smile, and even her teeth looked friendly.

"And you're wearing the same thing you always wear," said Liesl. The girl was wearing a collared shirt tucked neatly into khaki pants. She nodded, still grinning, which surprised me because Liesl's tone of voice sounded like a put-down to me.

"See you Monday at school, Leese."

"Yes, Kizzi, that's right," said Liesl, as if she were talking to a much younger kid.

Instead of being insulted, Kizzi just smiled even more as she walked away.

"Why were you talking to that girl like that?" Gareth asked.

"Like what?" Liesl asked.

"Like she's your pet dog or something."

"And you didn't introduce me or tell her I was going to the Gill Park Gallery School or anything," I said.

Liesl put her hands on her hips and glared at both of us. "She's always using big words like she's totally stuck-up."

"She doesn't seem stuck-up," said Gareth.

Liesl took off. Even with sandals on, she was fast. I had to work to keep up with her as we ran along the path through the woods.

I remembered the day last summer when Liesl had first brought me to Mitch's tree house. It had been hot then, but the trees in the woods had provided shade. Now I could feel the cool air coming into my lungs. The old leaves that were still on the branches rattled a bit in the breeze.

And then we were standing in front of Mitch's oak tree. I couldn't believe what I was seeing. The trunk was completely spray-painted blue. I felt anger boiling up.

Liesl opened a little door hidden in the bark of the tree and pressed a red button three times. "That's the signal that it's me," she said.

Liesl pressed a black button, and the plywood box that was the elevator came shaking and shivering down two metal rods that ran down from the tree house.

"On tray, silver plate," she said, opening the door. It was Liesl's way of saying, *"Entrez, s'il vous plait,"* which was French for, "Come in, please," which she'd learned from living with Belle Vera.

I stepped in and held my breath as we went up. I had never quite gotten used to the elevator, even though I'd been up and down in it a bunch of times. Even now I was wondering whether or not we would survive if it crashed.

It made it up this time. When it stopped and the door opened, I gulped with relief, and there was Mitch Bloom, all six feet of him, with his springy gray hair and his bobbing Adam's apple. I was so glad to see him. I guess he was glad to see me, too.

He practically lifted me out of the elevator. "Hey, Willy, my boy," he boomed. "You're like fresh manure for a tired plant!"

I looked around, happy to see Mitch's tree-house apartment again, the neat, shipshape way he was able to have a kitchen and a living room, a bathroom and a bedroom, all fit into a small space.

"It's terrible about those kids spray-painting your tree," I said.

Mitch nodded and sighed.

"Come on, Willy, you gotta see where I live," said Liesl. She tugged my arm, no longer Miss Cool Teenager.

"Take a look around Liesl's Palace," said Mitch. "And then come back down and we'll talk about the Blue Gang."

Mitch had added on a whole new level to the tree house for Liesl. I followed Gareth up a little ladder and then pushed up through a hatch door in the ceiling. This brought us outside to a staircase—right out in the air, with the rustling leaves all around us. It was a good thing the stairs had big railings on both sides, so it felt safe. Then we pushed up through another hatch door, and there we were, standing in Liesl's room. It was snug, with a bed and a chair and a rug on the floor. One of the windows had shelves built across it. They were filled with glass bottles of all different colors.

"In the morning the sun shines right in, and it looks like a stained glass window," Liesl said proudly. "That was my idea. Your aunt made the quilt, and Belle Vera made me the braided rug, and Mitch Bloom made my bed frame."

The quilt was a lot like the quilt on the bed I slept in at Aunt Bridget's, a patchwork of bright colors and funny shapes.

There were pegs on the wall, and Liesl's collection of cool and geeky clothes was all hung up. Even her shoes, including a pair of red sneakers, were lined up. The bed was made.

"It's so neat," said Gareth in surprise.

"Mitch Bloom makes me keep it like this," Liesl said. "He says a plant can't grow in a weedy garden."

She pulled back a curtain and showed us her bathroom. It was tiny, but also very neat.

The whole tree began to vibrate. I froze for a minute, and then I realized the elevator was on its way back down to the ground.

"Come on," said Gareth. "Let's go back down."

We heard the elevator coming back up, and then in a few moments Belle Vera was filling Mitch's living room with oohs and ahhs.

"Vill-ee!" she exclaimed. "To see you here, it is just like the good old days!"

While we had been looking at Liesl's Palace, Mitch had made tea and muffins. The smell of apple and cinnamon and nutmeg filled the room. Everyone helped themselves and then settled down in the living room, Belle and Mitch on the couch, the rest of us sprawled out on the floor. I took a bite of one of the muffins. It was warm and delicious, all full of little apple bits.

"Mitch, Willy says on the way into Gloria today he saw Dillon Deronda dressed up in a Blue Gang outfit," said Gareth.

"Ah, the species of coward, hiding his face like that," Belle fumed. "Why do not the police interfere?"

"I don't think they take vandalism like this that seriously," said Mitch. "But of course, the best thing to do is repair the damage right away. Most vandals are lazy, and after a while, they'll give up. But it's not so easy to get it off the trees," he added sadly.

Gareth sipped his tea noisily and took a huge bite of muffin. "The question is, *why* is Dillon doing this?"

"Ah, there it is, *pour quoi*," Belle said, nodding her head in agreement.

"Someone could go and *ask* him why," I said.

Everyone stared at me for a moment.

"What do you mean?" Liesl asked.

"I mean, wouldn't it make sense for someone to go and ask Dillon why he is doing this?"

Mitch threw his arms up in the air. *"Yes!"* he exclaimed. His Adam's apple bobbed enthusiastically. *"Yes!* That's it! It's a blooming fantastic idea!"

"*Moi,* I think so, too," said Belle, still nodding.

"Yeah, but who's going to go ask him?" asked Gareth.

"I could go," said Mitch. "But since he attacked my tree, he must be pretty mad at me about something."

"The three of us could go," said Gareth. "Willy, me, and the Queen of Cool."

"I don't think so," said Mitch. "He'd think the Gorillas of Gill Park were ganging up on him."

"One-on-one is the best idea," Gareth said, agreeing. "But it can't be me." He pulled on the visor of his baseball cap. "I doubt the Sharks' leading man is going to want to talk to the Gorillas' numero uno."

"Well, he hates my guts," said Liesl. "And it's mutual."

They all looked at me.

"He's not exactly crazy about me," I said. "He thinks I'm shark bait."

"Yeah, so you won't intimidate him. That's good," said Gareth.

"Thanks," I said.

They continued to stare at me. Liesl looked like a puppy who wanted a dog treat. Gareth's mouth was hanging slightly open. Mitch's forehead was pushed up into wavy lines. Belle was sitting as still as a statue, maybe holding her breath until I gave the right answer. I shifted uncomfortably. I could say yes and be the hero, but the thought of Dillon Deronda made my skin crawl.

Mitch got up and went over to his desk. He started to flip through the pages of a phone book. "Deronda. There are a ton of Derondas here. All on Smart Street." He was looking at me again. "I'm fairly sure Smart Street is in the South Park, the old section of town. It's made up of generations of brick-layers, masons, and carpenters. They are the people who built the city of Gloria, you know—rough but honest folk. Hey, Belle," he said, looking excited, "we might even get some of the Derondas to help build the oven. They probably know all about the bricks we'll need."

"Rough but honest," I echoed. "Great. I can't wait to go into *that* neighborhood."

"Good," said Mitch as if it were a done deal.

"But remember the sign Dillon had in the park last summer?" I asked. "He was looking for spare change because he was hungry. He's a runaway or something."

"Maybe," said Mitch. "But it's getting cold now. He's living somewhere."

No one spoke for a moment. I was able to hear music, a snatch of a chord here and there, but it was enough to make me think of Mr. Pettingill. He had entrusted the park to me, Willy Wilson, and a gang of kids was trying to wreck it.

"I guess I'll go," I said.

"That's our man," said Gareth. He leaped up from the floor, where he had been sitting, and gave me a friendly slug on the arm.

"Magnifique," said Belle, clapping her hands together.

"You are the sturdiest tree in the forest," said Mitch, his Adam's apple bobbing cheerfully.

Liesl didn't say a word, but she had a smile on her face, and her eyes seemed bluer than usual. My heart gave a little twist.

"No problem," I said.

five

Shaving your head is like
getting rid of clutter.
—Jack Mack

For supper Aunt Bridget ordered in Chinese food. We—meaning Mom, Aunt Bridget, Jack Mack, Zack Mack, Gareth, Liesl, and I—sat around the kitchen table eating. I was so happy to be in that cozy kitchen again, with the walls decorated with hats and canes and walking sticks.

At home we never ordered in. We always ate dinner in our dining room, or every once in a while in a restaurant at a table with white tablecloths and three hundred extra forks and spoons you never knew what to do with.

"I am honored to meet you, Willy Wilson," Jack Mack said to me. "I understand if it weren't for you, we wouldn't have a park anymore. Hope you don't mind sitting down to eat with a Shark." He nodded at Zack. It was funny looking at the two of them—Zack's hair was big and out of control, and Jack's head was shaved smooth as an egg.

"Howdy," said Zack with a grin. He'd always been an easygoing Shark. "Hear you're going to our school. You'll like Mr. Kim. He knows everything."

"He knows how to teach you, anyway, Zack," said Jack. "Never seen the boy work so hard in his life."

"He always worked hard at baseball," said Gareth. "Too bad you're on the wrong team."

"Maybe you guys can win him over to the Gorillas," said Jack.

"Yeah, that would fry Dillon all right," said Liesl with a laugh.

"I don't know," said Zack, pulling at his hair. "I'll have to think about that one."

Jack dumped one of the little cardboard cartons of rice onto his plate. "Dillon Deronda," he said, wrinkling his nose. "Bridget told me he's part of the Blue Gang. That kid always did give me the willies." He shook his head, looking at Zack. "I never did understand what you see in him."

"Zack likes everyone," said Aunt Bridget. "That's just how he's made."

I wondered then if I should mention I was going to go and try to talk to Dillon, but Jack Mack was already on to the next thing.

"Say, any of you kids want to be in a play? It's called *The String Man*. I'm holding auditions pretty soon. There are a lot of different kinds of parts."

Gareth frowned. "I'll have to look at my schedule," he said. "I have a ton of homework this year, and I'm on the varsity soccer team. But I could probably manage it. I'm pretty good at multitasking." He shoveled a shrimp into his mouth. With his braces gone, the food went into his mouth better than it used to, but he still was a messy eater.

"Multitasking!" Aunt Bridget snorted. "No one actually says things like that in real life."

"How about you, Willy?" Jack asked.

"I'd like to," I said.

"See what your workload is first, Willy," said Mom.

"You can try out, too," Jack said, turning to Liesl. "There are some great parts for girls."

"For cool girls or geeky girls?" Liesl asked.

"Actually," said Jack, "there's a monkey. Sister Monkey. She swings across the stage on a rope."

Liesl's eyes lit up.

Just then we heard thumping on the stairs, and then there was my father standing in the doorway, out of breath and looking excited. He was carrying a violin case. "Gareth's dad has been sorting through the final details of Mr. Pettingill's estate," he said. "I guess it has been a very long and complicated process because Mr. Pettingill was so thorough about details. Anyway, he left this violin to you, Willy. It's a Hans Zerbe."

Aunt Bridget and Jack Mack gasped and looked at each other and then at me. "A *Hans Zerbe!*" they said at the exact same moment.

"What's a Hans—whatever?" Liesl asked.

"Hans Zerbe is one of the foremost violin makers in the country, and he lives right here in Gloria," said Aunt Bridget. "Imagine that!"

The violin case somehow reminded me of Mr. Pettingill's face: It was old and weather-beaten, with lines and cracks in it. "Here, let's clear off some space," said Aunt Bridget. We swooped away the mess on the table, and Aunt Bridget followed with a sponge. I set the case down. *Click, click, click,* I snapped open the clasps and lifted out the violin.

"Whooeee." Jack whistled.

"It's lovely," said Aunt Bridget. "It just sort of glows. Oh my, Roger would have drooled over that." Not for the first time, I wished my uncle Roger, who had been a really good violinist, hadn't died. He should have had this violin. The front gleamed like reddish-gold honey. The back had little flicks of flames caught right in the wood.

I felt like the wrong side of a magnet—that if I reached out for that violin, it would jump away from me.

"Go on. Pick it up and try it," Dad urged.

"Hold on," said Aunt Bridget. "It looks like there's an envelope in there. It's addressed to you, Willy."

Sitting right on the red satin bed lining of the case was a small white envelope. Sure enough, it said, WILLY WILSON. I set down the violin and then picked up the envelope. Opening it, I pulled out a sheet of paper.

I ran my eyes down the page filled with scrawly handwriting and saw Mr. Pettingill's signature at the bottom.

"Hello, Willy," I read out loud. *"I'm not here anymore, in body, anyway, but I hope that my spirit lives on in Gill Park and also in this violin, which I bequeath to you. Perhaps as you draw the bow across the strings some of my spirit will materialize like a genie out of a bottle."*

I stopped reading for a moment. I felt breathless. It was so strange to be reading a letter from Mr. Pettingill. It was as if he had come to life and had walked right into the room.

"Go on," said Dad.

"Ah, Willy," the letter went on, *"it was my good fortune that you came to Gill Park this last summer of my life. Now you are the owner of the park, a precious set of green hec-tar-es—"* I stumbled on the word, not knowing what it meant. He always did have a way of talking to me as if we were on the same level.

"A hectare is equivalent to about two and a half acres," said Dad. "Keep reading."

"You, Willy," I went on, *"who understood what a patch of green in the middle of a city could mean, you will be a good steward. Ah, Willy, what stroke of good fortune sent you this way? Life is a mystery, is it not? And furthermore, there is a mystery in Gill Park, one that I would like you to solve. It involves treasure."*

"Treasure," Gareth echoed. I glanced over at him. The freckles on his face seemed to shimmer, a sure sign he was excited.

"Yes, Willy, my boy, I am sending you on a treasure hunt. Here is a rhyme for you to help you on your way:

> *"These clues you will follow*
> *As you fly like a swallow*
> *There is treasure to be found*
> *And you'll find it, I'm bound."*

Aunt Bridget put back her head and laughed. "That old scamp! As sick as he was at the end, he still had fun."

"What's the treasure?" Liesl asked.

"I don't know," I said. "He doesn't say."

"There must be a clue," Gareth said. Both he and Liesl were trying to grab the letter out of my hand.

"Stop it," I said. "I can't read it."

"Here is a clue for the first part of the chase: You must go and look at the stare-case," Gareth read.

"But he misspelled *staircase,*" said Dad, who was also breathing down my neck.

Gareth went on. "He also says, *'There is only one rule to this hunt: Wherever you go to find the clue, you must not ask directly about the treasure. Otherwise, you will be DISQUALIFIED!'*

"A treasure in Gill Park," said Gareth. "That is so cool. When are we going to start?"

"We could start right now," said Liesl.

"Well, Willy," said Dad, "before you go gallivanting off somewhere, your mother and I need to be saying our farewells. It's time for us to be getting home."

There was a lot of scraping back of chairs and people standing and saying good-bye to my parents. Gareth punched me on the arm and said, "Later, buddy," and Liesl and Zack both said, "See you in school on Monday."

When everyone was gone, Dad started pacing around Aunt Bridget's living room. Mom stood completely still. "You still have the list, don't you, Bridget?" she asked. She'd written out a long list of stuff I was supposed to do.

"Right on the fridge," said Aunt Bridget.

"We think you should stay here on the weekends at first, Willy," said Dad. "Let you get used to homework demands and so forth. We'll come out and visit you as often as we can. But just because you're here, don't be wasting all your time looking for that treasure," he added, as if he could read my mind. "Treasure can wait."

"And you be good for that young Mr. Kim," Mom said. "Do your homework, and don't forget about the violin. Oh, Bridget!" My mother started looking frantic again. "I forgot all about finding a new violin teacher for him!"

"Don't worry, we'll look into it," Aunt Bridget said, patting Mom's arm.

Mom wrapped her arms around me and kissed me, and then they were gone.

Aunt Bridget tucked a strand of hair behind her

ear and blew out a big breath. "Phew," she said. "That wasn't too bad. Your mom held up pretty well. Are you okay, Willy?"

"I think so," I said. "It's hard to tell. Am I really me? Am I really here? Am I really going to a different school?"

Aunt Bridget nodded in an understanding sort of way. "It will take a while to adjust, I'm sure."

I looked at her, suddenly feeling shy. "I'm . . . It's . . . You're . . ."

"You're worried about being in my way," she said, nodding again. She put her hands on her hips and looked at me seriously. "Now listen here, Willy. Your uncle Roger and I were planning on having about ten kids. Well, as you know, life seems to have had a different plan in mind." She glanced over at the photograph of Uncle Roger she kept on top of one of her bookcases. "But now, see," she said, turning back to me, "I get to borrow you for a while. And you know what, Willy? One of *you* is wonderful!"

I swallowed hard and looked down at my feet.

"Tomorrow's Sunday," said Aunt Bridget. "You'll have the whole day before you have to go to school on Monday. You can take Roger's bike and ride around the park all day, if you want to."

"Good idea," I said. After all, I had to go and find Dillon and talk to him, and the sooner I got that over with, the better.

six

A good pitch, she is like making a good sauce—
you start with the fresh ingredients and
you hope it has the zest and the zing!
—*Lena Deronda*

The next day I set off for Dillon Deronda's on Uncle Roger's old bike. I didn't tell Aunt Bridget I was going to see Dillon Deronda. I don't know why. Maybe I thought she would try to talk me out of it, and I'd lose my courage.

With a street map stuck into one of my pockets, I rode across the park, heading for the south side.

In Mr. Pettingill's apartment a musician was playing Vivaldi on the violin. I was proud I could recognize a lot of composers now, and that was because of Mr. Pettingill, too.

Up ahead I saw Old Violet, the homeless old woman, sitting on her bench. Now she was wearing what looked like a couple of old coats and a bright purple scarf around her head. You could never pass her without her screeching something at you. Sure enough, as soon as she spotted me, she opened her mouth. "HA! That you, Willy Wilson?"

I stopped and waited, elbows on the handlebars of the bike, feet resting on the pavement. I noticed, with a jolt, that there were blotches of blue spray paint all over her bench.

"YOU OWN THIS PARK, DON'T YOU?" she asked, still screeching. I nodded. "THEN YOU DO SOMETHING ABOUT THAT GANG." Her little eyes gleamed like a pair of glassy marbles. Then her mood seemed to shift, and she broke into a huge grin. "Hey, did I tell you about my boyfriend?" She pointed to her dentures. I remembered them from the summer. They had always seemed so out of place with the rest of her. "My boyfriend gave me these teeth. You do something about that gang," she said, her mood changing again.

I climbed back on the bicycle and started to pedal away.

"YOU DO SOMETHING ABOUT IT QUICK!" she yelled after me.

I reached the South Park and, hopping off the bike, pulled the street map out of my pocket and studied it. I needed to go down Grant Street four blocks and then turn right on Smart Street. *Smart Street!* It figured Dillon would live on a street with a name like that.

The trees on Smart Street were big, like they'd been growing there forever. The houses were crowded up against each other like a bunch of friends waiting in line. White steps led up to bright red or yellow or green doors. Each house had a little garden out front. One was full of little gnomes and elves and mushrooms. Another still had rosebushes blooming in it. A dad walked by, pushing his baby in a stroller. A little boy trailed behind, singing a song to himself.

I was coming to the end of the block when I saw a man sitting in a wheelchair right in the middle of the sidewalk. He was wearing a gray sweater and holding a plastic yellow bat in one hand, slapping it against the palm of his other hand.

"Hello," I said, slowing down, thinking he must be a baseball fan.

"Huh," he growled at me.

"I'm looking for Dillon Deronda," I said.

"Well, you won't find him here," the man growled again. He slapped the bat harder against his palm.

"But do you know where he lives?"

"Ha-ha," was all the man said.

His eyes were narrow, and he had a pointed face. I knew that face. I was sure he was related to Dillon in some way. "Look," I said, "it's important. I need to talk to him."

"What are you, the FBI? You on some important

42

assignment?" He laughed a mean, dry laugh. My stomach churning, I started to ride away. "Number eighty-two," he shouted after me. "Doesn't live with me no more. He's too good to live with his own father." I looked back. He was waving the plastic bat in the air over his head.

As I was crossing the street to the next block, the music started up again—first two flutes, and then two violins, and then a man's voice, and then a woman's. The two voices chased each other, a sort of conversation, or was it an argument? They weren't singing in English—I'm pretty sure it was Italian. But even though I couldn't understand what they were saying, their voices soared along, smoothing the worry right out of me. I hopped off the bike and started walking, pushing the bike along, listening.

The house numbers were in the eighties now, and then I saw a small woman standing in her yard. As I got closer, I could see she was wearing a pink-flowered dress. Behind her was a bush of huge pink flowers looking almost exactly like the flowers on the dress. The whole scene looked like a painting, especially as the woman was standing so still, holding on to a rake, her eyes shut tight, and this angel-like smile on her face. The house number was 82.

I called out, "Hello," not too loud, not sure if I should disturb her.

Her eyes flew open, and at the same moment the song ended. She stared at me, but didn't seem to see me, and then she shook her head. "Ah, the music, she is so beautiful." An even bigger smile beamed across her little face. Her cheeks were like two more bright pink flowers. She held out a hand and cupped it, palm up. "I would hold on to that singing if I could. Those two voices—that's a miracle!" She took a step closer, and I could see she looked older than she had looked at first. A million lines crinkled in her face. "I think it is Puccini they are singing." She spoke with an accent. I guessed she was Italian, too. "My mama and papa, they sing such songs when I was a child. Now that Mr. P. has passed on, we hear opera sometimes. That is a good, a very good thing."

I felt a beat of pride. It had been my idea, after all, to have Mr. P.'s apartment become a place where people could sign up to rehearse and try out their music for the public. "I'm looking for Dillon Deronda," I said.

The woman plumped her hands around the rake. "You come here to see Dillon?" she asked, surprised.

"I'm hoping . . ." I stopped, not knowing what to tell her. "I play baseball. I thought I'd just—"

"Baseball?" Her face wrinkled into smile lines. "Ah! You know who teach him to pitch like that?"

I shook my head.

"Lena Lionatti Deronda." She pointed to herself. "I am Dillon's grandmother. When Dino, that's his father, is hurt, I teach the boy. Hours and hours we play because I see the talent in that boy. And now when I watch him pitch, it makes me happy, so happy!" Her flower cheeks turned even pinker. "We take him in, Leo and I. He doesn't want to live with his father no more, after . . . after . . ." She stopped, shook her head, her face looking sad now. "Is okay," she went on. "You don't need to hear this bad story. I don't know you, do I? You are a friend? My Dillon, he does not have many friend."

"I'm Willy Wilson," I said. "I played baseball in the park last summer." I didn't know how much to tell her. She must have seen the games, and maybe she'd eventually recognize me as being on the team that beat Dillon's team, but now she was just nodding as if I were a total stranger. "Okay if I go in and talk to him?" I asked.

"Yes, of course!" she said, beaming. "A friend for my boy, a nice-looking boy like you, a good friend for my Dillon. Come, I show you."

I followed Dillon's grandmother up the steps to the door. She was small, but she was quick and wiry. It wasn't such a stretch picturing her teaching Dillon how to pitch. She pushed open the door, and we stepped into a dark and gloomy hallway.

"Carrisimo!" she shouted up a narrow stairway. As my eyes adjusted to the dark I could see paper here and there peeling off the walls. The carpet running up the stairs was fraying at the edges.

"What do you want?" Dillon's voice, snarly and rude, came down the stairs.

"A boy, a friend, is here to see you," Dillon's grandmother shouted. I was glad she hadn't mentioned my name.

We heard thumping upstairs. "Ha!" she exclaimed cheerfully. "He is coming." Smiling, she patted my arm and went back out the door.

I stared up the staircase, waiting for Dillon to appear. *Staircase,* I thought, thinking of Mr. P.'s clue. But then there Dillon was, coming down the stairs, with his pointed face, his little eyes, his sharp chin, his long hair back in a ponytail. He was wearing a black T-shirt and a black pair of jeans. He took one look at me and stopped on the third stair from the bottom, not too close.

"Oh, it's *you,* Shark Bait," he spat out.

Then I did something I'd seen my father do when he was greeting someone. I stuck out my hand, leaned forward, reached up. I looked the rat-face square in the eyes. "Hey, Dillon," I said. "What's up?"

Dillon couldn't help it. He grabbed on to my hand just for a second before he flung it back as if he'd been stung. He looked like he might hit me. "What do you want?" he asked, blinking his little eyes.

I don't know why I said what I said next—the words were just there, sitting in my mouth. "I want you to help me find the treasure," I said.

seven

Everyone knows life ain't a fair deal, but if it was, Frank Featherstone would be sitting where I am, and I'd be sittin' where he is.

—*Dino Deronda*

"The *what?*"

Dillon looked completely startled, as if he'd been struck by lightning. He stood with one hand on the banister, tight and tense. "Just what kind of *treasure* are we talking about?" he asked slowly.

I was startled, too. I hadn't expected him to be interested.

"Mr. Pettingill set up a treasure hunt just before he died," I said, the words rushing out. "There are clues and everything."

"Mr. Pettingill!" His body slumped. "Yeah, right, like his idea of treasure would be some kind of fancy violin."

I bit my lip, thinking of the Hans Zerbe. "No," I said. "I don't think so. I don't know what it is. Maybe it's gold or something."

Dillon studied me for a moment. "You don't have any idea?"

I shook my head.

"So," he said finally, "why are you telling me about it? We're not exactly buddies."

I took a breath and plunged in. "You're smart," I said. "I figured you could help me find it."

I saw a flicker of something in his eyes. "What's the first clue?" he asked.

I cleared my throat. "I'll tell you—on one condition."

"What could that be, I wonder?" Dillon asked, a nasty smile curving his lips.

"You have to stop wrecking the park," I just managed to say.

Dillon smiled his mean smile again. "How do you know it's me?" he asked.

"I saw you."

"Maybe I have a twin," he said.

I squeezed my fists tight. "Why would you want to wreck things in the park? Don't you play baseball in it?"

Dillon looked surprised. "Hey, it's not my park. It's your park." He pointed a finger at me, stabbing it in the air. "It's all the rich people's park."

"I'm not rich," I said.

"Maybe not, but you *are* the owner." He narrowed his eyes, making them even squintier. "Listen, man, there are two kinds of people in this world—the guys who get what they want; they're on this side." He sliced the air with his right hand. "And then there are the punks who don't get anything." He made a fist with his left hand. "They live right here." He punched the wall. "And it's not like I need the park. I can play baseball anywhere. I'm out of here in a few years. My pitching arm's going to win me a ticket to any place I want to go."

I sighed. "Why are you wrecking the park?"

"Maybe I'm not wrecking things," he said. "Maybe I'm looking for treasure, too." He raised his eyebrows, and for some reason, I felt prickles on the back of my neck. But then he rubbed his hands together. *"Treasure,"* he whispered in a mocking voice. As he turned and started walking up the stairs there was something about his shoulders, the way they hunched over, that made him seem not so tough. I swallowed hard and yelled after him.

"I'll give you my e-mail in case you change your mind."

"My grandparents don't happen to have a computer," he said without turning around.

"It's gillparkgorillas—" I started to say.

"Are you sure it isn't losers?" he interrupted, grinning at his own hilarious humor. "Now you get out of here. I don't know how you found me, but I don't want you here, you understand?" Then he went up the stairs and disappeared. I could hear the slamming of a door.

As I went out the front door I could see Dillon's grandmother kneeling in the yard, gloves on her hands, digging with a trowel. Around her were bright orange flowers in pots.

"Did you have a nice talk?" she asked as I came down the steps.

"Great," I lied.

"Not so great," she said quickly. "That poor boy. So smart, he is, and once so eager for the world. And then the accident." She shook her head and pulled off her gardening gloves, peering at me intently. "You look familiar. What is your name again?"

"I'm Willy," I said, trying to be patient. I was worried about Dillon coming out and finding me still standing in his yard.

"Well, Willy, I tell you about Dillon's papa. His name is Dino. Dino, he was on the ladder, three story up, fixing the window in one of those houses, you know, the ones that Frank Featherstone buy around here for five dollar and sell for five hundred thousand dollar." She shook her head sadly and then went on. "Three story up Dino is when he fall."

I bit my lip. That old batty guy in the wheelchair really was Dillon's father. "I'm . . . I'm sorry," I said. "That's terrible."

Dillon's grandmother nodded. "Terrible," she agreed. "And after the accident, Dino, he turn sour, like the milk you keep too long. No, nothing is the same after he fall off that ladder. He, Dino, he make the life not so good for his family. His own wife, Dillon's mama, she leave. I cannot say I blame her, but this is sad, very sad for Dillon. He is still only a young boy. And then, he, Dino, he does the very bad thing." She took a deep breath. "He steal the *tesoro*."

"*Tesoro*," I repeated. "*Tesoro* . . ."

Tears were falling now, down her crinkled pink cheeks. "*Tesoro*. 'Treasure,' you say in English."

"Treasure," I repeated. "What treasure? What do you mean?"

The front door opened. Dillon appeared on the top step. He saw me and, with a yell, leaped down and started running toward me, shaking his fists. "Get out of here, Willy Wilson, get out of here, and don't ever come back again."

"Dillon, *carissimo*, what—"

"Get out of here—"

"Forgive him, he is— *Dillon,* why are you—"

I grabbed my bike and started running. It wasn't until I was halfway down the street that I managed to scramble up on it. Then I realized I was heading straight for Dillon's father, who was still sitting smack in the middle of the sidewalk. Heart pounding, I crossed the street, pedaling like I was escaping a fire.

"Hey! Where you going so fast?" I heard him yell. "Did you find him? Did you find that no good louse of a son? Won't even live with his own flesh and blood—"

I kept my head down and didn't look up until I almost smacked into a car door that was opening just as I rode by. I dodged just in time, and then stopped, catching my breath. The car was a long black limo. A uniformed driver was walking around it to the other side. He leaned down and opened the back door, and a tall man in a blazer unfolded himself out onto the sidewalk. I blinked for a moment, not believing my eyes. I was almost positive it was Frank Featherstone. I took off, the blood in my veins fizzing like I'd had too much sugar.

When I reached the park, I got off the bike and leaned it against a tree. I sat down on a bench and tried to think. "Maybe I'm looking for treasure, too," Dillon had said.

Had Dillon been making fun of me? Or had he been talking about the treasure—the *tesoro*—his father had stolen?

eight

After I painted my fingernails black,
other kids stopped picking on me.
—*Robby Wildman*

On Monday morning I made sure I left for school extra early. I didn't want *Mister* JinYoung Kim yelling at me the first day.

I hopped on Uncle Roger's bike, an old pair of Uncle Roger's gloves on my hands and one of his scarves wrapped around my face.

As I reached the east side I came out of the park and walked my bike along the sidewalk, my stomach churning. And there was Kizzi sitting on the front steps in a bright blue down jacket and a bright blue hat. I breathed a little easier. If she was just sitting there, I wasn't late yet. As I crossed the street she said, "You must be Willy. Mrs. Vera, she called to tell me you were going to be a new pupil at our school," she said in that crisp, polite way of hers.

I could see a large scar just below her right eye. She saw me looking and touched her fingers to it. She unfolded herself and stood up. "Welcome to our school," she said with a big smile.

"Thanks," I said. I couldn't help grinning back. I was trying to imagine Kyle McNulty or Cody Harris standing at the front door of my old school greeting a new kid like this.

"Look," she said. "Leese is coming. She is being cool today." Her bright face brightened even more.

Sure enough, Liesl was coming down the street. If I hadn't known her, I might not have recognized her right away. She was wearing a short blue-jean skirt, a leather jacket, stockings on her legs, and high heels. Her hair was curled, and she was wearing lipstick and black stuff all around her eyes.

Liesl came right over and formed a hand into a fist and socked me on the arm. I noticed she was wearing all those rings on her fingers again. "Hey, Willy Wilson, you're here. That's so cool."

"And *you're* cool," I said.

"Come on," she said. "I want to show you around before the others show up. Oh, too late, here comes Wildman."

Wildman was a big, tall kid wearing a long black trench coat. He had a buzz cut, which made his cheekbones jut out.

"Yo, you must be the new kid," he said, turning in my direction. "Greetings from the Black Avenger." He held up a hand, every fingernail painted black. Then he turned toward Liesl and stared at her for a moment. "Hey, Liesl," he yelled in a way-too-loud voice. "How come you have baby snakes all over your head?"

Liesl had a blue vein just above the bridge of her nose. It lit up like a warning when she was about to lose her temper. She glared at Wildman.

Zack came bounding up the steps. "Knock it off, Wildman," he said.

"I don't need you to say that, Zack Mack," said Liesl, still acting very cool and collected. "I can defend myself. Don't listen to anything Wildman says," she added, turning to me.

Wildman grabbed my arm. "Hey, Willy, you into Black Avenger at all? I have all the Avenger games if you ever want to come over." He stretched and yawned. "I stayed up 'til two last night and almost got to level four, can you believe it? Pretty impressive, huh? But then Gran woke up and caught me and threatened to put me out in the street if I didn't go to bed."

"Willy, my man!" Zack greeted me with a high five. He was wearing baggy pants, a baggy sweatshirt. His hair was just as wild and curly as ever. His clothes and his hair seemed too big for his skinniness.

"So," said Liesl, hands on hips. "We're all here except for Gabriela, who is always late."

"There she is," said Kizzi. "And Fernando is with her."

"Oh, that's just super-dandy," said Liesl sarcastically.

"Her little bro," Zack explained.

"I think he's cute," said Kizzi.

"He's a brat," said Liesl sharply.

"Not any worse than you are," said Wildman.

Gabriela came slowly toward us, wearing a jacket with a fuzzy collar. Fernando was wearing a brown sweatshirt. He looked as if he wasn't warm enough.

"*Vámonos, apúrate,* Fernando, come *on,*" Gabriela said as Fernando dragged limply behind her. Her voice was spicy sounding, with just a hint of Spanish in it. Her large dark eyes flashed with frustration. "He has to come with me today. It's a day off at his school. I told him he has to keep his mouth shut, and no whining."

"This is Willy. He's going to be going to school with us," Kizzi said. "This is Gabriela."

"Hi, Willy," Gabriela said with the nicest smile I'd ever seen on a girl. I stood up a little straighter. "And this is my little brother, Fernando," she added, nudging the little boy with her elbow.

"You forgot Ernesto," the little boy said, still hanging on to Gabriela. "You didn't tell him about Ernesto."

Liesl rolled her eyes, ignoring him.

"Ernesto," Fernando said in a louder voice. "Ernesto Peligroso. He is right here." He pointed to empty air. "You didn't tell his name. He is going to come to school with us, too."

"Come *on*," said Liesl. "We're going to be late, and Mr. Kim won't like that."

She stepped through the heavy front door to the entrance hall, and we followed. Itsuko Furukawa, the curator of the museum we had met on Saturday, was sitting behind the counter. I couldn't help staring at her. Today her eyes weren't green at all. They were yellow.

"You better get going. You're going to be late," she said.

"Come on, it's Monday, black square day," said Liesl. Immediately everyone started hopping or leaping or just stretching out a leg and only stepping on the black squares of the marble floor. Fernando was laughing his head off. Liesl made for the staircase.

"Ernesto wants to keep playing," Fernando said, crossing his arms and standing still on a black square.

"Come on, Nando, we have to go," said Gabriela.

"No, he wants to play," said Fernando again.

Liesl marched down the stairs, strode over to him, and stuck her nose right in his face. "I'm going to tell you something, Fernando. And you can tell Ernesto for me. This is a very old building. And guess what? There are prehistoric insects who live in this building. If you are very quiet, you can hear them chewing. Shhh. Listen."

Everyone was quiet. There seemed to be a steady humming coming from somewhere—not exactly a chewing sound, but Fernando's eyes grew big and round.

"They are here, everywhere, big old cockroaches and termites with giant jaws that chew and chew. And guess what? This is a school, not a play yard, and when you're in a school, you work and you study and you learn. And if you don't, those old cockroaches and termites will come out of the walls and chew both you and Ernesto *alive.*" Fernando's mouth fell open. He found Gabriela's hand, put his own hand in it, and didn't say a word.

"Thank you, Liesl," Gabriela whispered as she followed her up the stairs.

"No problemo," said Liesl.

nine

If I could live inside a painting,
I would always be safe.
     —*Zio Aguilar*

The big, burly guard was standing on the landing in front of the elevator again. His dark eyes lit up when he saw us.

"Mornin'," he said. "Got the new one with you today, I see."

"Yup," said Liesl. "Name is Willy Wilson. This is our guard, Zio. He makes sure nobody scribbles stuff on the paintings."

Zio saluted me. "Howdy, again. You'll like it here," he said. "It's full of beautiful paintings. I never get tired of it. Never."

I found myself staring at Zio. He reminded me of a little kid, but at the same time there was an old look in his eyes that didn't match the rest of him.

Then Liesl led us into the room where we had met Belle and Mr. Kim on Saturday. Mr. Kim was standing at the far end of the table, a stack of notebooks in front of him. He looked so serious. My stomach did a little lurch.

"Good, we'll begin now," he said. The other kids pulled notebooks from the pile and sat right down and began working, everyone except for Gabriela and, of course, me. I didn't know what to do.

Gabriela approached Mr. Kim, looking worried, while Fernando dragged on her arm. "Mr. Kim, I'm sorry, I had to bring my little brother with me. I'm really, really sorry."

"Tell him about Ernesto," Fernando whispered.

"No," Gabriela whispered back fiercely, blushing hard. "I'm not going to do that."

Mr. Kim stooped down slightly to speak to Fernando. "Take the drawing material," he said very quietly, pointing to a stack of paper and several boxes of colored pencils on the table, "and sketch one of the paintings in this room."

"Why?" asked Fernando.

"Why?" Mr. Kim looked surprised. "I'm so glad you asked. *Y* is the twenty-fifth letter of the alphabet. It comes from the Semitic letter VAW. So, incidentally, do the letters *F, U, V,* and *W*. The Greeks called it *upsilon.* The Romans turned it into two letters, *Y* and *V*. Aren't you glad to know that?"

Fernando's mouth dropped open.

"Now," said Mr. Kim. "You must not talk, and you must let the students work."

Fernando hesitated a moment.

"Cockroaches," Liesl hissed under her breath.

Fernando scuttled like a scared bug and sat down at the table. He reached over and took two pieces of paper off the stack. "You draw, too, Ernesto Peligroso," he whispered to the air beside him.

Then Mr. Kim turned to me. "I'll determine where to begin with you pretty soon, William. In the meantime, you draw, too."

"Me, draw?" I felt stung, as if I were a little kid like Fernando and had to be kept busy. I realized Mr. Kim must have brought the drawing materials for me.

Mr. Kim waved a hand at the paintings on the wall. "Look, William, we are in an art museum. There are many paintings here. I can't get to you right away. So please take in what you see. Choose a painting to draw while I'm working with the others. Go on, William, stand up, walk around, look."

I got up and walked over to a painting. It was embarrassing, but pretty quickly I realized the other kids weren't looking at me at all. They were working away. Even Fernando was completely into what he was doing. I guessed Ernesto Peligroso probably was, too.

I was standing in front of a painting of scenery, these high cliffs with this little thread of a river winding through them at the very bottom. The trees on the cliffs were amazing, made up of all these little feathery flecks of paint. People had been patient back in the old days before cameras. I wasn't that patient. I wouldn't be able to draw all that.

The next one was of a lady with a head full of wild red hair. She had a fierce expression on her face, and she was holding a paintbrush up like a dagger. There was a pair of white shoes on a table just in front of her. She was painting her own face on the shoes. The little plaque next to the painting read SELF-PORTRAIT OF MERLA.

I glanced over at Fernando's drawing. He was copying a painting of a bowl of fruit and a vase of flowers. He was doing a pretty good job. Great. A six-year-old, or however old he was, could draw better than I could.

Mr. Kim was explaining something to Zack. Zack pulled on his hair, making it stand up even more than usual, and chewed on his pencil. Mr. Kim sat down beside him. "Your eyes play tricks, you know, Zack. They see a plus when they should see a minus. So take your highlighter and be sure to highlight the plus or minus before you try to operate. Highlighting will help you see better."

He moved around to Kizzi and watched her for a moment. She was writing and erasing, writing and erasing. She finally sighed and rested her chin in her big hands and looked up at Mr. Kim. "For some reason I am not calculating correctly," she said.

He bent down and looked at her paper. "Try centimeters," he said.

She stared at her page and then broke into a

huge smile. "Oh, *centimeters*," she said, and started working again.

Mr. Kim went over to Liesl. Her tongue was stuck between her teeth, and I could see she was concentrating hard. Glancing over at what she was doing, I almost flipped. Liesl, who had never been in a school before in her life, was already doing long division. I thought about the struggles I had with long division, lining up the numbers, remembering all the steps.

"You're making good progress, Liesl," said Mr. Kim. "You're a very bright girl with numbers. Numbers are like candy to you. You eat them up." Liesl's face broke out into a huge grin. Mr. Kim smiled back at her. Wow! What a smile! I didn't think he'd ever smile at me like that.

Liesl looked back down at her work. The pencil in her long fingers flicked like a magic wand across the paper.

And there was Wildman working with Gabriela. They were drawing these perfect triangles using a ruler. Everyone was working on something except for me.

Okay, I had to try. I took a step closer to the Merla painting. Her expression was sort of a challenge. "I dare you," she seemed to be saying. I slapped my piece of paper on the table.

Well, to start with, I drew the frame. I'd try to fit everything inside of that.

Mr. Kim glanced up from his work with Wildman and Gabriela. He saw what I was doing. He nodded, and then came over and stared at the painting for a minute. "See how the lines make the room go back? That is perspective, William. That is math. Now notice the geometric shapes. What is a rectangle, what is a square, what is a circle? It will make drawing so much easier." Just a hint of a smile crossed his face. A quarter inch maybe. "The pencil will help you see."

Feeling encouraged, I took another look at Merla. "Yeah, you can do it," she seemed to be saying.

Merla's face was kind of a rectangle. Her cheeks were circles. I started to draw.

Now in the silence I could hear all the thinking going on in the room. The air was thick with thinking.

Mr. Kim passed by. "This is good, William," he said to me. "You're seeing now, really looking. Here. You can rest your paper on this so you can get up closer." He handed me a book.

I pulled my chair over and sat smack in front of the painting. I started drawing Merla's hair and eyes and nose and mouth. I tried to capture her fierceness. It was kind of weird she was painting her own face on the shoes, but then, in the end, I had to admit I liked her weirdness.

I was surprised when Mr. Kim said, "Okay, time for the next class." I rubbed the back of my neck. It ached from the way I'd been craning my head up to look at the painting.

Liesl came over. "Let me see your drawing," she said. I pulled it away from her. "Come on," she said. She snatched the paper out of my hand and held it out so she could look at it. "I like the way you drew the shoes," she said. "They look like birds." Her voice was bubbly, full of laughter.

"Oh, thanks," I said.

"But it's good, Willy, it's good. I mean, don't get all huffy and bent out of shape."

I sighed and climbed off the chair. A little bit of Liesl went a long way. Was I really going to like going to school with her every day? The mascara had rubbed off, so she had big circles under her eyes. And actually, Wildman had been right about her hair. It did look like dead snakes now, with all these limp strands hanging down around her raccoon eyes.

Belle Vera came into the room and plumping her hands on her hips said, *"Bonjour, mes enfants."* Everyone seemed happy to see her. Kizzi went right over and hugged her. Then Belle turned to me, beaming, and came over and kissed me, French style, on each cheek. "Vill-ee," she said so warm and nice. "You are here! It is a marvel, a miracle! Now tell me, what language is it that you would like to study?"

"I can choose any language at all?" I asked, not quite believing my ears.

"Any language at all," Mr. Kim said.

"How about . . . about Italian?" I stammered. I was thinking of Dillon's grandmother—how if I learned Italian, I could really have a conversation with her.

"Ah, *benissimo!*" Mr. Kim exclaimed. "And I shall teach you myself." His mouth curved up, and his eyes disappeared into two straight lines. I couldn't help it—I was seeing everything in geometric shapes now. "I admire a boy who tries new things!"

I felt a rush of happiness. I'd go to school with Liesl 24-7. It was so worth it to be in a school like this.

ten

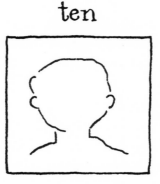

I can beat up anybody who tries to hurt
Fernando's mother or his sister.
—*Ernesto Peligroso*

I'd been going to the Gallery School for a few weeks now.

I liked a lot of things about the school—the other kids, for one thing, and our elective time for another. Twice a week we could spend the afternoon learning anything we wanted to. At first I thought about taking violin lessons, but then I decided to study famous staircases in Gloria, hoping I'd find the first clue to the treasure hunt. I hadn't found the clue yet, but so far I'd learned a lot about the architecture of the Gloria Opera House, the Gloria Courthouse, and a bunch of old houses.

Another thing I liked about the school was Itsuko Furukawa. She taught a course in art history twice a week. I looked forward to it every time. She let us look at paintings, and then we talked about them.

But Mr. Kim . . . Mr. Kim was hard, and nothing I ever handed in to him was good enough. He put red marks all over everything I wrote.

"I have been seeing editorials in the newspaper about how terrible the vandalism is in the park," he said to me one day. "You are the owner of the park, William. You must learn how to write forceful prose so you can defend it."

That was when I made the mistake of saying things were hard for me because I had ADD.

His eyes lit up, and you could almost hear the little bell go off in his brain. "*D!*" he exclaimed. "*D* is the fourth letter of the alphabet. It represents a voiced dental plosive, or stop. You pop your tongue against your teeth to make the sound like this: 'duh,'" he said in an exaggerated way, showing me his tongue and his teeth. "And in Roman numerals, *D* stands for the number five hundred, and that's how many times you should revise your writing until you get it right."

So the weeks went by, me liking most things about my new life, even though Mr. Kim still made me feel nervous and I still hadn't found the first clue to Mr. P.'s treasure hunt. Before I knew it, it was almost Halloween.

Aunt Bridget was standing at her ironing board

pressing a piece of shiny red material. A number of people had hired her to make their kids Halloween costumes.

"What about you, Willy? What are you going to be for Halloween?"

"You don't think I'm too old?" I couldn't help asking her. If I had been at home, I knew Mom wouldn't have let me go out trick-or-treating.

"Of course not," she said.

"Well, I have this idea," I said.

Aunt Bridget laughed. "Don't make it sound so unusual. You often have ideas."

"Gareth and I think the Blue Gang is going to use Halloween as an excuse to trash things in the park, so I was thinking we could get our Gorilla baseball team to be guards."

Aunt Bridget held up the material she was working on and shook it out. It looked like a long red cape. She set it carefully over the back of a chair and then, shifting some stuff off another chair, sat down opposite me. "So, you're going to try to stop the Blue Gang from doing whatever they're doing?" she asked. "Won't it be a problem, though, if they see you?"

I cleared my throat. "I was thinking of the gorilla costumes you made last summer that we used for the team. You made almost thirty, didn't you?"

Aunt Bridget nodded, making a face at the memory. The gorilla suits had shed black fuzz all over everything.

"Well, we'll be gorillas for Halloween. And we'll

carry cameras so if the Blue Gang does anything, we'll be able to take pictures of them. People who don't have cameras can get those disposable ones."

Aunt Bridget's face lit up with a huge grin. "That, Willy, my boy, is a stroke of genius."

"Do you still have the gorillas somewhere?"

"Of course. I figured you might need them for your team next summer. My neighbor Ann Moriarty has a shed she lets me store things in."

On Saturday morning we met beneath Mitch's tree. The whole team was there. It was great to see all the guys, especially Capasso, Toenail, and Dixon. They crowded around me, too, slapping me on the back, telling me what a great idea I had about going into the park as gorillas. Toenail, who used to have blue hair, didn't have any hair at all anymore. He'd shaved it completely off.

"My mom made me do it," he said. "She thought everyone would think I was part of the Blue Gang."

"Hey, guys." Strolling toward us was Zack Mack, looking as if he'd been part of the Gorilla team all his life.

"So," said Gareth, not entirely friendly. "Are you a Gorilla now?" You could feel the tension in the other Gorillas.

"Heard there might be a bit of trouble in the park tonight," Zack said in his easygoing way. He took out his harmonica and blew a few notes. "Thought I'd try to help you guys out." He played a few more notes.

Gareth looked him up and down. "You up for wearing a gorilla costume?"

"Just this one time," said Zack with a grin.

"Only thing," I said slowly, "is what Dillon will think about it."

Zack Mack shrugged. "One gorilla looks pretty much like the next gorilla. What Dillon doesn't know won't hurt him."

We saw Liesl walking toward us with Kizzi, Wildman, Gabriela, and Fernando.

"Thought we needed more people," Liesl said in a businesslike way. She was wearing a red sweatshirt and jeans and red high-tops. Her old tonsil-colored cap was crammed down over her eyes.

"This here is Kizzi," she said, flicking a thumb in her direction. Kizzi giggled slightly. "Robby Wildman in the trench coat," she continued, pointing.

Wildman put up his black-nailed hand.

"Gabriela is with the little brat—I mean brother— and his name is Fernando."

Gabriela looked around, taking everyone in with her warm smile. "Hi, guys. Hope you don't mind if we help out," she said in her spicy-sounding voice.

Gareth stepped forward. "The more the better," he said seriously.

"I could dress up like the Black Avenger," Wildman said. "I have a wicked cool outfit."

"Listen, Wildman," Liesl said. "You already look like the Black Avenger, and we're being gorillas. I told you that."

"You forgot Ernesto," Fernando said. "You always don't tell about Ernesto. Ernesto," he said in a loud voice. "Ernesto Peligroso. He is right here." He pointed to empty air. "He's going to wear a gorilla costume, too."

"Hey, Ernesto," said Gareth, reaching out and shaking an imaginary hand. "Good to meet you. Glad you could come. Hope we can find a suit that fits you."

Fernando shouted with laughter and looked at Gareth like he was his hero. "So," said Gareth after a pause, "we'll pick up the gorilla costumes at Bridget McTaggart's. If you don't know where it is, just ask Willy here. And everyone needs to bring a camera and a flashlight."

"And a bag for candy," said Liesl. "I'm not going to miss out on the whole candy thing because of Dillon Deronda."

"Do we get to fight the Blue Gang?" Wildman asked.

"Ernesto Peligroso will get 'em!" Fernando yelled excitedly, punching the air with his fists.

Gareth shook his head. "We don't have to do anything but act like we're regular kids out trick-or-treating. But then if something happens, we take a picture, but we don't hang around. Next day we develop the pictures and send them to the newspaper."

"I say we ride bikes," said Zack Mack. "We'll cover more territory and get away faster."

"Right," said Gareth.

"Ernesto can't ride a bike," Fernando piped up in a small voice.

"You mean *you* can't?" Liesl asked meanly.

Fernando hung his head. Everyone looked away. I had the impression we were all thinking the same thing: No one wanted to be stuck with a little kid.

"He can ride in front with me," said Wildman.

"Thanks, Wildman," said Gabriela, her eyes big and grateful. The rest of us looked down at the ground, feeling guilty but relieved.

"Okay, guys, meet us at Bridget McTaggart's house for the gorilla costumes, seven o'clock sharp."

Wildman saluted Gareth. "At nineteen-hundred hours, right-o, Captain."

Just as it was getting dark we ran out of Aunt Bridget's house, all fifteen of us—well, sixteen if you're going to count Ernesto Peligroso. Aunt Bridget had been good with Fernando, making sure his gorilla suit fit. She had even made a big fuss over Ernesto Peligroso, holding a suit up in the air, saying that it was too small because Ernesto Peligroso had such big muscles.

It was great to be a gorilla again, and this time it wasn't sweltering hot, and we weren't about to face the Sharks in the final play-off of the season. Of course, in a way we *were* facing the Sharks again, and it was more important—the stakes were higher.

As we crossed the street I heard a voice. "Look at all the gorillas, Mommy!"

As soon as we ran through the gates of the park, I

pounded my chest out of pure excitement. I was out in the dark this Halloween, not inside passing out candy like I would have been at home.

Gareth had brought his video camera. He pointed it at me, and I rolled on the ground, the leaves crunching into my fur. The fountain lights came on, and at that same moment a lone clarinet sounded a long, high note, high like Fernando's voice, but not so whiny. Then it broke into a fast and dizzy riff. One of the taller gorillas put out its arms, held up its head, and started dancing. Another gorilla joined in, doing pretty bad ballet.

Pretty soon we were all leaping around in the colored lights, and then someone flung an arm across my shoulder. In a moment we formed a circle, and then we were dancing around the fountain like we were at a gorilla wedding.

eleven

When people are mean, it makes my toes hurt.

—Kizzi Ngnoumen

The clarinet playing came to an end. As we gathered, Wildman brought out a rolled-up piece of paper. "I hope you guys don't mind, but I devised a strategy. Here's a map of the park." He unrolled the paper and spread it out on one of the benches. "See, I've marked it into quadrants and then subdivided each one into A and B. I figured we could pretty much work in pairs."

No one seemed to mind that Wildman had taken charge. Kizzi and I were assigned to the northwest, area B. We headed out on our bikes, and pretty soon we left the lighted, paved sidewalks for the darker woods. Once there, Kizzi and I hopped off the bikes and sat down on a pile of fallen leaves behind one of the bigger trees. I pulled off my mask. The air felt cool against my face. I was glad to be in the warm gorilla suit.

We sat facing each other in the dark.

"How do you like our school?" Kizzi asked. I couldn't help smiling. Even in a gorilla suit Kizzi couldn't help being polite.

"I like it, although Mr. Kim is the hardest teacher I've ever had," I said. "How about you?"

"It's a very good school," Kizzi said in that crisp, slightly English accent of hers. "The people there are very kind. I could not learn at my other school, because I was afraid."

"Afraid?"

"I was beaten up." Kizzi's voice shook a little.

"That's terrible," I said, at the same time straining to hear if someone from the Blue Gang might be coming. I clutched the disposable camera, afraid of losing it.

Kizzi cleared her throat. "You see, I came from a very strict school in Nigeria. We had to be very polite all the time. We had to stand up when the teachers came into the room. When I came to school here, everything was different. I could not seem to get along with the other girls except for one named Alice, and no one in the class liked her either. I don't really know why. She dressed differently, maybe more like a little girl, and sometimes she brought a doll to school. The other girls laughed at her." She cleared her throat again. "Anyway, Alice was allergic to perfume. In homeroom the teacher made an announcement. 'Don't wear perfume because it makes Alice sick.' Some of the girls were angry. They thought Alice was making up the whole thing to get attention. There were two girls especially who were angry. They drenched themselves in perfume and stood next to Alice to see what would happen."

"Yikes," I said. "What *did* happen?"

My eyes had grown used to the dark, and I could see that Kizzi had pulled her knees up and wrapped her arms around them. "Alice had an asthma attack," she said so quietly I could barely hear her. "She couldn't breathe. She had to go to the hospital."

"Was she okay?"

Kizzi nodded. "She was out of school for an entire week, but in the end she was okay. Even so," she went on, "the girls still didn't have any sympathy. They thought she was pretending to be sick just to get them in trouble." She stopped talking for a moment. I listened for sounds, but there still didn't seem to be anyone coming. I was beginning to wonder if by being here in the woods we were going to miss all the action. "So then there was a meeting of the entire class," she started up again. "The teachers were trying to determine who the girls were that wore the perfume. Everyone knew but would not tell. Even Alice would not tell."

The ground felt hard where we were sitting, even with the leaves. I shifted around. "So then what happened?" I asked.

"So I told," she said. Her voice sounded shaky again.

"So they beat you up?"

"Yes," she said.

"What grade were you in?"

"Sixth grade. Last year."

"But you're tall. You must have been taller than—"

"They took me by surprise. They kicked and scratched. I still have a scar under my eye. I didn't know how to defend myself."

I nodded. I had noticed the scar—it was hard not to. "That stinks," I said. "What happened to the girls? Did they get in trouble?"

"No one ever found out. My parents wanted to come in and tell, but I wouldn't let them. I was too afraid."

"There wasn't anyone who would stand up for you?"

"No, everyone was afraid," she said.

I tried to take in what she was saying. I was wondering if something like that could happen at my old school. And what would I do? The kid code was pretty tough sometimes. You didn't rat out other kids.

"What made you tell on them in the first place?" I asked.

Kizzi sighed. "What they did was so mean," she said. "More than mean. They could have killed her, I think." She reached over and touched my arm. "Thank you for letting me tell this story. I have never told anyone before—not anyone except my parents."

Before I could think of what to say, I heard leaves crunching and then laughter.

"Okay," I whispered. "This is it."

Something came whizzing over our heads. It sailed up in the branches above us, gleaming white, twisty, and trailing—toilet paper. If that was the worst thing that happened, it wasn't going to be so bad. We heard the sound of more laughing and then the hissing sound of spray paint.

"Come on!" I grabbed Kizzi's arm again. "Get your camera."

We left the bikes and, darting from tree to tree, followed the sound. Just ahead we saw a bunch of shadowy bodies. They seemed big. I leaped forward, raised my camera, and clicked. In the flash of light, a gorilla face blazed up out of the darkness. I almost dropped the camera. One of the bodies started pounding its chest. Then they all leaped away, laughing, spraying paint over everything.

"What was that?" Kizzi asked, standing completely still. She pulled the mask off her face. I couldn't see her clearly, but I could hear the confusion in her voice. "Was that Gareth?"

"It wasn't Gareth," I said. I kicked a tree. "It was them. The Blue Gang. They dressed up like gorillas. They beat us at our own game."

I turned, groping along the trunks of the trees, looking for the bikes. I found them, picked mine up, and wheeled it along slowly. Kizzi followed without saying a word.

As we neared the fountain I stopped. Here and

there the colored lights of the fountain caught a hairy black arm, a gorilla face, a hairy black leg lunging out for a kick. There was shouting, grunting, swearing, hairy arms grabbing on to other hairy arms. How did anyone know which side anyone was on? One gorilla arm pulled back and punched another gorilla square in the middle of its face. And then there were bright lights, more shouting, whistles, and cops swarming all over the place. For a split second all the gorillas froze, and then they scattered, running in all directions.

"Come on." I grabbed Kizzi's arm. "We don't want to be caught here. Let's go." I swung onto my bike and headed for Aunt Bridget's house, hoping that Kizzi was right behind me.

When we burst into Aunt Bridget's apartment, she and Jack Mack were at the table, sitting there looking as calm as could be, their faces just poking above stacks of fabric.

"Did you have a good time?" Aunt Bridget started to ask, but a pounding on the stairs interrupted her. The door burst open, and a few more gorillas piled into the room. Gareth stood breathless, mask in hand. Zack Mack, Capasso, Toenail, Wildman, and Fernando were behind him, gasping for breath. Wildman's nose was bleeding, and his gorilla suit was ripped across the shoulder.

Jack Mack and Aunt Bridget sprang up from the table. "What in the world—?" Jack started to ask, but there was more pounding on the stairs, and the room became crammed full of gorillas. As the masks came off, we could see the rest of the boys from the baseball team, plus Liesl and Gabriela.

Gabriela looked wildly around the room. When she saw her little brother, she blurted out, *"Gracias a Dios,* Fernando, you're safe!" She grabbed him and burst into tears.

"They tried to kill Ernesto Peligroso," Fernando cried out in a shrill, little voice.

Everyone started talking at once.

"They were in gorilla suits." "They attacked Wildman." "No, Wildman attacked them." "I didn't even get a chance to video them."

Aunt Bridget stuck two fingers between her teeth and whistled shrilly. Everyone was quiet. "Take the gorilla suits off, all of you," she said. "And everyone calm down. And Wildman, or whatever your name is, come into the bathroom and I'll get your face cleaned up. Then we'll talk."

twelve

I could live without a telephone. I never like talking to people I don't know, and telephone poles are a waste of trees. But where would birds sit if they didn't have telephone wires?
—*Bridget McTaggart*

The next day was Sunday, and my parents drove out to see me. Mitch Bloom, Liesl, and Gareth came over to Aunt Bridget's, too, bringing the newspaper with them. Jack and Zack Mack were already there, Jack at the table with the script of *The String Man* smooshed in between Aunt Bridget's piles, Zack sprawled next to me on the floor. We were both trying to do homework. Aunt Bridget was picking up gorilla costumes from a heap near her feet and hanging them on a small rack set up next to Flora.

Mitch read the headline out loud. "GORILLA WAR- FARE IN GILL PARK." He rolled his eyes and went on:

> *"Kids dressed up like gorillas had a Halloween party in the park. Toilet paper festoons every available branch; every bench now has the telltale signature of the Blue Gang on it. Fires were set in trash cans. Young children were accosted by gorillas and fright- ened as they crossed the park to trick-or-treat. Police broke up a number of gorillas who seemed to be fight- ing amongst themselves, but the hooligans dispersed before police could catch them."*

"And listen to this," Mitch said, looking at another section of the paper. "Here's an editorial:

> *"Judging from the number of growing problems in Gill Park, one can't help but ask the obvious ques- tion—should a mere boy be in charge? Perhaps it is a sign that the park land has, after all, outlived its pur- pose. There is great need for development in this city. Free enterprise has come to a standstill. Potential retail space is taken up by a park that has become a playground for juvenile delinquents.*
>
> *"And is there, we'd like to know, some connection between last night's gorilla warfare and the Gorillas of baseball fame?"*

"I'd like to know who wrote that," Gareth said angrily.

"What *I* want to know is where the Blue Gang got the gorilla costumes," Aunt Bridget said.

The phone lying on the worktable rang. Grabbing it, Aunt Bridget kept shaking her head as the person on the other end talked. As she clicked off, she said, "That was Ann Moriarty. Her shed was broken into and a lot of the gorilla costumes were taken. Confound those brats!" She put the phone on the table and pulled a twisty thing off her hair and shook it loose.

"Brats?" Jack said, grinning. "Only you would call them that."

"I'll go over later and take a look," said Aunt Bridget, catching her hair back into the twisty thing again. Then she picked up another gorilla costume and hung it up. "That boy Wildman sure made a mess of his suit."

The phone rang again. Aunt Bridget answered it again. As she listened, she waggled her eyebrows and then handed me the receiver. "It's the mayor," she whispered.

Everyone in the room perked up.

"Hello," I said nervously, feeling butterflies in my stomach. I went and sat on the couch next to Mitch. "This is Willy Wilson."

"Ah, yes, Willy," the mayor said. "I'm glad to find you. I thought you might be at Bridget McTaggart's this weekend. Your park seems to be experiencing some problems."

"Yes," I said, not sure what to say next. The

mayor's voice sounded somewhat familiar, like a TV news anchor or something—very smooth and confident.

"When Mr. Pettingill willed the park to a minor, that being you, of course, Willy"—the mayor laughed slightly before continuing, although I wasn't sure what it was he thought was so funny—"I'm sure he didn't foresee that the park would become a playground for juvenile delinquents."

"Mr. Mayor, I—"

"You may, strictly speaking, be the owner, but the park, by its very nature, by its very location, is a public space, and as such, the city has a responsibility to protect those who pass through it, such as young children." There was an edge to the mayor's voice now. I found myself gripping the phone. "And it's my responsibility to you, Willy, to let you know that you're vulnerable. Yes, you're really opening yourself up to all sorts of trouble. Before you reach your majority, you're going to be mired in lawsuits up the wazoo."

"Mr. Mayor, I—"

"I know, strictly speaking, the park is in the hands of a board of trustees and that you, as a minor, are not really in charge."

"I—"

"I'm trying to put it to you as clearly as I can, Willy." I clenched my teeth as he went on. I was beginning to feel like a squished-up, run-over ant. "I owe it to you to spell out the hard truth. This park of yours is going to have to be shut down if your board can't manage it."

"Shut down?" I asked. I got up off the couch.

Aunt Bridget, Mom, Dad, Zack, Mitch, Jack, Gareth, and Liesl were now circling me like I was on a sinking ship and they were lifeboats trying to rescue me.

"Tell him you can't talk right now," Dad mouthed.

"Tell him it was Dillon Deronda!" Liesl was almost shouting.

"I'll talk to him," said Mitch, trying to reach for the phone.

The mayor seemed to be droning on about how perhaps the park wasn't worth all the trouble it was causing. Then he said, "If I were you, Willy, I'd think about your college education."

"My college education?"

"Prime piece of real estate," said the mayor. "Put yourself through college and then some."

"I . . . I can't talk right now," I finally managed to say. I pushed the END button. I could feel my heart bump in a sickening way.

Before I could put the phone down, it rang again. I just about jumped through the ceiling.

Taking the phone from me, Aunt Bridget answered it. Her eyes widened, and she sort of staggered to the couch and sank down. "Just a moment," she said. She stuck her hand over the receiver. "He says he's the mayor," she said. "But he sounds different from the other mayor."

"Jumpin' Jiminy," said Liesl.

"I'll take it," said Dad, reaching for the phone.

"Then who were you talking to, Willy?" Liesl asked.

"I don't know," I said, my pulse still bumping away. "Whoever it was said he could shut down the park. He said I should think about selling it."

"Man," said Zack, whistling through his teeth.

We all turned to listen to Dad's conversation. He was pacing around the room and he kept saying, "Yes, right—right, I agree." He didn't seem upset, just serious. "Yes, good. Thanks for calling. We'll be in touch."

He put the phone on the table and jammed his hands into his pockets and started jingling the coins in them. "Well, that really was the mayor," he said.

"How can you be sure?" Aunt Bridget asked.

"Oh, I've known Fred for a long time," said Dad. "And he said while he didn't think the problems last night were more than the usual Halloween non-sense, he'd like to help in any way he can—put more police on duty around the park. He says he recognizes how valuable it is to this community and appreciates all the work being done on it." He looked at Mitch. "Mentioned you in particular, Mitch."

The phone rang again. "Could someone else get that, please?" Aunt Bridget looked at the phone as if it might bite. Liesl sprang for it. "Hello. Oh, you're from the *Gloria Times*? Wow! Willy, it's a reporter!"

"Tell him he's not—" Dad was shaking his head.

"Yeah, he's here," said Liesl. She stuck the phone in my face before I could think.

"Hello," I said weakly.

"Tell him about Dillon," Liesl whispered loudly.

"Hi, this is Tom Flannigan with the *Gloria Times*. Is this Willy Wilson?"

"Yes," I said.

"You certainly must be upset about what's happening in the park," he said.

"Yeah, yeah, I'm—"

"Is there some time I could come over and interview you?"

"Dillon and the Blue Gang," Liesl continued in her loudest whisper. "Now's your chance."

"Tell him you'll talk to him later!" Dad was getting mad.

I told the reporter I couldn't talk right now. He said he'd call me later in the week. I put down the phone.

"Don't talk to anyone else until we've thought this through, and definitely don't talk to anyone unless you can see their face," said Dad. "Who knows who'll be on the other end?"

I felt a twist in my stomach.

"Dad," I said, turning to him. "Do you think the guy who said he was the mayor could have been Frank Featherstone?"

Dad raised his eyebrows, which were thick like Aunt Bridget's—and mine, for that matter—a Wilson family trait. "Well, I wouldn't put it past him. Did you recognize his voice?"

I shook my head. "That's just it. I wasn't expecting it to be him, so I wasn't thinking about it, and I only heard Frank Featherstone speak one time. All

I remember was that it was kind of a tight, snobby voice, and I guess maybe this guy's voice was, too, but I couldn't swear to it."

"I think you should send that reporter a written statement," said Dad. "Something to the effect that you have every intention of preserving the character of the park in the spirit of Otto Pettingill; that you know that the people of Gloria fully appreciate having green space in the midst of their city; that it is a place where people of all ages can come to rest and play; that being outside is nicer than being inside; that you welcome ideas for improvements; and that in the end, the vandals are only hurting themselves, and everyone knows it."

I looked at my father wondering if I would ever be even half as smart as he was.

thirteen

When I miss the Old Country, I walk in
the park, and I think, *the sky is the same
sky, the grass is the same green.*
—Leo Deronda

Mom and Dad spent Sunday morning going through
my schoolwork with me, looking at all of Mr. Kim's
red marks. They didn't say much, but they sighed a
lot. I could tell they were worried they might have
made a mistake in sending me to the Gallery School.

"I think I'll just ride around the park," I said to
Aunt Bridget after they left. Maybe listening to Gill
Park music would make me feel better.

"Good idea," she said. She reached into the big
orange bag she always carried around with her and

pulled out her wallet. "And if it wouldn't be too much trouble, maybe you wouldn't mind stopping at Rosa's and picking up some food for supper." She handed me a twenty-dollar bill.

I grabbed a jacket, and then I was off on Uncle Roger's bike. As I crossed into the park, music coming from Mr. P.'s apartment cheered me right up. It was a Brazilian samba played on a guitar.

And then I thought maybe I'd just wander over to the South Park and ride up Smart Street. Maybe Dillon's grandmother would be outside, and I could just casually get her talking. In no time she'd be telling me all about the family treasure.

No one was in the front garden at Dillon's grandparents. Of course not, it was the first week of November. All the leaves were down, and it was *cold*. No one was going to be out *gardening*.

So now what? I needed courage. So what if Dillon came to the door? What could he do to me, anyway? Well, he could punch me in the face. I perched on the bike, feet on the pavement, debating. *C'mon,* I told myself. I finally walked up the steps and rang the doorbell.

The door opened. It wasn't Dillon. I figured it was his grandfather, a small old guy with white hair. He was wearing a blue shirt and a gray sweater-vest and dark blue pants. And then Dillon's grandmother stepped out and joined him. She had on the same pink-flowered dress I'd seen her in the last time.

"Who's there?" the old man called out.

I stepped up a little closer. "It's me, Willy," I said

to Mrs. Deronda. "I came by a few weeks ago. Do you remember me?"

Mrs. Deronda peered at me, and then she broke into a smile. "Oh, it's you. Yes, of course. I am surprised to see you after my grandson shout so much at you. But maybe you know inside he is not so bad." Before I could say anything, she said, "Mitch Bloom come to our house the other day. He think maybe it is our Dillon who is doing the bad thing to the park."

"Our Dillon!" Mr. Deronda said. "He has no proof of such a thing!"

So Mitch had come here, probably not long after I had told him how my trying to talk to Dillon hadn't worked out too well. Dillon would see it as me ratting him out.

"Is Dillon home?" I asked nervously, trying to see past them into the dark hallway.

"No, no, he is not home," said Mrs. Deronda. "He work for his uncle Gino. Gino, he is helping Mitch Bloom to build good things for the park. So I try not to be angry with Mitch Bloom. He is not a bad man. He has good ideas, no? Now there is no baseball, we try to keep Dillon busy. Keep him out of trouble."

"I wondered . . . I wondered if I could ask you some questions."

"Some questions?" Mr. Deronda looked doubtful and suspicious. He took a step closer to me, his brown eyes looking me up and down.

"The other day . . . the other day you were talking

about the family . . . the family treasure," I said to Mrs. Deronda.

"Ah!" she said, nodding. "The *tesoro,* yes, I remember. I start to tell you."

"You tell him about the *tesoro*?" Mr. Deronda turned to her in surprise.

"This is a good boy," said Mrs. Deronda. "He play baseball, he make good friend for Dillon, he listen to my stories."

"But you don't even know him!"

"My name is Willy Wilson," I said. "You might have heard of me. I . . . Mr. Pettingill, when he died, he left me the park."

Mr. Deronda's hands flew up to his face. "Oh, *Cristofero Colombo*! You are *that* boy! And you must have so much concern for what is happening in the park. You do not think it is our boy?"

Before I could answer, Mrs. Deronda said, "You come inside, Willy." She grabbed my arm and squeezed it hard. "And you call me Lena."

"And you call me Leo," said Mr. Deronda, reaching out to grab my other arm. For such a frail-looking old guy, he had a pretty firm grip.

Between the two of them, they practically lifted me off the ground and carried me into the house.

They pulled me down a hall into the kitchen. I looked around. It seemed like a pretty old kitchen. The wallpaper was faded, and the linoleum on the floor had a scrapy, worn-away look. The refrigerator looked like one you'd see in a 1950s *National Geographic* magazine. Still, the room was bright and cheerful, with flowers in big pots on the windowsill above the kitchen sink and a bright yellow plastic tablecloth on the table.

There was a big photograph of Dillon on one of the walls. He must have been in first or second grade when the photo had been taken, and he wasn't looking mean yet. He was wearing a baseball uniform, grinning this really cute grin with his two front teeth missing.

"Sit down, sit down," said Leo, pulling out a chair. I sat down at the table while he cleared off newspapers and coffee mugs.

"Get him something to eat, Leo," said Lena. "I make something to drink."

I sat down while the two old people bustled around. Lena pulled some lemons out of the ancient refrigerator and started slicing them in half. Leo reached into a large glass jar that was on the counter. He pulled out some long, cookie-looking things and put them on a plate.

"Go on, have some, from Rosa's Market, *biscotti*," he said, putting the plateful down in front of me. "We save them for special, like this, a visit from Willy Wilson."

I tried one. It was good—sweet, but not too sweet, crumbly and crispy. I thought about my own grandparents, Mom's parents, the only grandparents I knew because Dad's parents had died before I was born. When I went to their house, we never sat in the kitchen like this. We always sat in the living room and had tea and cookies. The cookies were always the same—thin and yellow and a little soggy.

"You a baseball player, too, huh, Willy?" Leo said as he sat down at the table across from me. "You play for the Gorillas, I remember. You make that last home run."

"That was just luck," I said. "I'm not good at baseball like Dillon is. He's good enough to be in the pros someday."

Leo's brown eyes lit up his leathery face, and his whole face shone. He nodded in a trembly way. "Lena and I, we think he is good enough. If he doesn't go to jail first. See, we don't know," he added with a sigh. "He has the anger inside him—much, much anger. It might be true, what Mitch says, that he is doing this bad thing to the park. We hope is not true, of course. Lena and I, we try to teach him the right thing, but is not easy."

"I already tell Willy about Dino and the accident," Lena said. She had squeezed the lemons into a glass pitcher, and now she was stirring sugar into it.

"Yeah, I'm real sorry," I said.

"Dino, Dillon's father, he never want to do nothing after that," Leo said. He spread out his arms and shrugged. "Who knows why some people, they hide from life's problems. We all got problems, I tell him. You're not the only one."

"And then he steal our *tesoro*," Lena said. She banged an old metal ice tray into the sink. Ice cubes popped out, some on the floor. She stooped down to pick them up. "How he could do that?"

I took another bite of the biscotti, and then I took the plunge. "Can you . . . can you tell me what the treasure is?"

"Santo Francesco, you know him?" Leo asked. It sounded like he was asking if I knew his next-door neighbor. "You call him Saint Francis."

"Saint Francis," I said. "Yeah, maybe I have heard of him. Something to do with animals?"

"That's right," said Leo, nodding. "He is born rich, you know. His father sell the fine silk, and for many year, Francesco, he live like a rich boy. He wear the fine clothes, he buy what he like. But then one day he get rid of it all. He give away his fine things. He say he will live like the poor. He wear only a brown robe, not smooth, but rough." Leo rubbed his thumb against his fingers as if feeling the roughness of the cloth. "He walk without the shoes. He sleep under the beautiful, starry sky all the night." He held a trembling hand up, palm flat over his head. "No roof, only the starry sky. And Francesco, he is a friend to everyone."

Lena began pouring the lemonade. "He say, all living thing, they are his brother, they are his sister. Let the *limonada* sit now, just a *momento,* while we tell you about the *tesoro.*"

"In the town of Assisi, in our country, they build a beautiful basilica to honor Francesco," said Leo.

"A basil—?" I asked.

"Like a grand church," said Leo. "It is where they put the body of Francesco. For by now Francesco is one of the greatest men in all of Italia, in all the world. He is a saint! And the great painter of Italia, the great Giotto di Bondone, he come and paint the pictures inside the basilica. He tell the stories of Santo Francesco's life." He leaned toward me. "Do you know Giotto?"

"No, I don't think so," I said, sorry to be letting him down again.

"A great painter, a very great painter." Leo spread his arms wide. "They say Giotto, he change the way people paint forever. And it is my ancestor who mix the colors for the master Giotto. And it is also he who make the plaster on the walls where Giotto paint," he added proudly.

"One day," Leo went on, "my ancestor take a little of the color that he mix, and he paint his own painting, his own little Santo Francesco speaking to the birds. Maybe he is not so good as the great Giotto, but is from the heart, you understand? My ancestor, he paint the picture on a piece of wood." He used his hands to show me. It was about the size of a small book.

"The treasure!" I exclaimed, finally getting it.

"*Sì, sì, exactamente!*" Leo pounded the table with his fist.

"You drink now," Lena said. I took a sip. It was really good. She watched me. "Is okay?" she asked.

"It's great," I said. "Really. I've never had real lemonade like that before."

"*Grazie, carissimo,*" Lena said with a smile. She took a sip and also smacked her lips. She pushed the plate of biscotti toward me. "Have another," she said.

I did. It was great with the lemonade.

"So," Lena went on, "the papa pass this small painting on to *il figlio,* the son, and when the son grows to be the papa, he pass it down, and on and on, it is passed on."

"Seven hundred year it stay in *our* family." Leo pointed proudly to his chest.

"Seven hundred years. Wow!" My mouth fell open.

"Even when our family come to America, to Gloria, the painting come with us. My mama, on the ship to America, she walk on the deck with the painting hiding inside her dress!" Leo laughed. "Just in case there is a problem, no? And now, after seven hundred year, the painting, she disappear."

"One day Dino say to Dillon, 'Take down the painting, Dillon, I want to see it up close,'" Lena leaned toward me as she continued the story. "Because he is in the wheelchair, no? So Dillon, he take down the painting." She pointed to a place on the wall where the painting must have hung. There was only a small rectangle now, lighter than the rest of the wallpaper. "And the next day, Dino, he say it is stolen, but I know that it is *he* who steal the family *tesoro*—"

"One day he has no money to buy the beer, and the next day he has plenty of money and plenty of beer," Leo said, trembling so hard now he could not hold his glass.

Leo and Lena looked so sad I didn't know what to say. And that's when Dillon walked into the kitchen.

There was this moment of silence, like the air around us suddenly froze. Dillon just stood there and stared at me.

"What is he doing here?" Dillon finally said.

"Dillon, *carissimo*, come in, sit down," said Lena.

I felt braver knowing that with his grandparents right there, Dillon probably wasn't going to punch me.

"I told you not to come around here." Dillon narrowed his squinty eyes at me. I glanced at his school photo, at the happy, open face.

"I'm just leaving," I said, scraping back the chair and standing up. "Thanks for the lemonade and everything," I said to Leo and Lena.

Then my brain did a little jump. For some reason I thought of Jack Mack's play. I took a deep breath.

"I actually came to see if you would audition for a play," I said. "Zack Mack's dad is directing it."

"A *play*?" Dillon looked at me in disgust. "Are you joking me?"

"He'll pay you." I was feeling reckless. "If you get the part, that is. He's looking for someone to play Tazan, the king of this tribe that's always going to war."

That made Lena and Leo laugh. "Just the part for you, Dillon," said Leo.

"Jack Mack is holding auditions Friday night," I said. "Over in the North Park at the new Art Factory. Seven o'clock." I looked Dillon right in the eye. "Be there or be square."

I called out thanks again to Lena and Leo, and then I bolted for the door.

On the way back to Aunt Bridget's, I stopped at Rosa's Market and bought spaghetti, tomato sauce, and biscotti.

fourteen

I keep my glasses clean and my wig on
straight, and the only complaining I
do is on Monday mornings.
—*Wanda Wojtkielewicz*

During one of the breaks on Monday, Belle came
and asked me if I would go out on an errand. Someone needed to go out and pick up some glasses
they'd ordered for Zack, and Zack couldn't go,
because he was still taking a test.

Zio was on the landing as I went by. He grabbed
my arm and stopped me. "You study hard and you
stay in school," he said. A dark look seemed to fill his
eyes. "I left school when I was fourteen. Lived on the
streets. Played cards to make money. Three-card

monte, all day long. Got good at it. Four years I lived like that. Then I went into the army when I was eighteen to get off the streets. You study hard."

I took a deep breath and nodded. "I will," I said.

He let me go, and I raced down the stairs, jumping three at a time, and leaped across the marble floor, being sure only to touch the black squares. It was a black-square day.

"Hey, Willy," said Itsuko. "You leaving?"

"Not for long," I said.

"Good, I wouldn't want you to miss art history class."

That reminded me. "Do you know about Giotto?" I asked.

"Of course I do. And the Italians are my favorite. Yours, too?"

"I don't know, but I thought maybe I could learn more about Giotto."

"You have good taste," she said. A man and a woman came into the gallery and approached the counter. "Got to work now. See you later, Willy," she said.

Outside, I let my fingers bump alongside the iron railing as I walked down the street. I was going to Wanda's Wigs and Glasses on Royalston Street. I crossed the street and walked three blocks in and two blocks over, and there it was.

The bell on the door jangled as I pushed it open. It was a little store, not very well lit, and no one seemed to be at the counter. Cases lined the walls, and in the cases were rows and rows of frames. I stepped closer. I could see that behind each pair of frames was a piece of cardboard. Eyes had been painted on the cardboard—not only eyes but eyebrows and eyelids and eyelashes and the bridge of a nose where the glasses rested. All those details gave the eyes different expressions. Some were staring; some looked surprised; some were excited; some were mad. There were laughing eyes, and maybe flirting eyes. One pair was winking. Someone, I thought, had had fun making all these eyes.

A small woman with short, blonde hair appeared from a back room and stepped up to the counter. "Hello, darlin'," she said cheerfully. "What'll you want from Wanda today? Wigs or specs?" Her voice was deep and scratchy but warm, and she was smiling a plastered-on, red lipsticky smile. She was wearing glasses, too, big ones with bright red frames, and a lot of gold jewelry around her neck. Behind her was a shelf of Styrofoam heads with faces painted on *them*. They were all wearing glasses and wigs.

"Could I—just look at everything for a minute?"

The woman—I guessed she must be Wanda— laughed. "Of course you can. Many people admire my stare-cases—yes, that's what I call 'em, my stare-cases. Cunning, don't you think?"

"*Stare-cases?* You really call them that?"

I wanted to run or leap or shout or climb over the counter and give Wanda a big hug.

"Yes, indeedy, I do." She checked herself out in a small hand mirror that was lying on the counter.

"About the stare-cases—" I started to ask.

"My store is like an art moo-zeem," Wanda gushed. "It's listed in the top twenty-five sights to see in Gloria. Wanda's Wigs and Glasses is number sixteen. Yup, it's just like an art moo-zeem, a must-see." She chuckled again. "A must-*see,* but first you gotta buy a pair of my glasses so you *can* see."

"Did you paint all those eyes?" I asked.

"Who, me?" She pointed to herself with a bright red fingernail, bracelets dangling off her wrist, and sounded amazed. "Listen, darlin', I couldn't paint myself out of an eyeglass case. This is the work of Merla."

"Merla!" I exclaimed.

"Yes, darlin', Merla. It might surprise you, but she's a dear friend of mine. We went to school together, back in the days before she got all famous. Then we worked together in a shoe store. Yup, selling shoes. That was my first job, and hers, too. That's where I got my taste for retail, but Merla went on to other things. Merla isn't her real name, of course." She raised her eyebrows and lowered her voice and looked over her shoulder as if someone might overhear. "Her real name's Sally Simpkins. She always did hate that name."

"By any chance, did you also know Mr. Pettingill, the owner of Gill Park?" I was trying to think about how to fish for the clue without coming right out and asking her about it.

"Did I *know* him? Why, darlin', he was not only my *customer* for forty years, he was also one of my dearest friends. We played bridge together every Thursday night for almost forty years. I'm the one who got him to branch out in his musical taste. I mean, Mose-Art and Bok and Shoe-Bert, those fellows are okay some of the time, but a steady diet can make you feel kind of down, don't you think? A little jazzamatazz, I'd say to Otto, is what this town needs."

"Did he get his glasses here?" I asked.

"Oh, yes, darlin', he came here for his first pair of specs, came here for his last. Coughed and coughed that day he came in. Such a shame."

"Do you still sell any of the frames that Mr. P. might have bought?" I asked. I thought they might, somehow, get me closer to whatever it was I was supposed to be looking for.

"Oh, yes, I do, right here, darlin'."

She pointed to a row in a case to my left. I recognized the thick, dark frames. They were so familiar, as if some part of Mr. P. were sitting there.

"But what in the world is *that*? A patch?" Wanda came out from behind the counter, and then I saw what she was looking at. One of the eyes had a patch on it.

"That's awful peculiar," she said. "I never noticed that before, but then, I don't dip into this case that often. Come to think of it, he's about the only one who ever bought this style—not too much in fashion these days." She took a little key that was attached to one of her necklaces and opened the case. Using a pair of red fingernails like a pair of tweezers, she pulled the patch right off. "Well, look here," she said.

"There's a little note all folded up and tucked right here behind the patch." She extracted the note and unfolded it. "Well, I'll be the bee's knees. Someone's gone and written up a little poem in tiny little handwriting. I'll need my specs for this one to be sure."

"I'll read it," I said eagerly.

"Be my guest," she said, handing me the piece of paper. Sure enough, there was Mr. P.'s scrawly handwriting in such small letters I almost needed a pair of glasses myself to read it. I read out loud:

"Wanda's specs are so fine and new,
That you see me and I see you.
Here you are at Wanda's stare-case
What could be next in this great chase?
Go see my friends from England olde
Many a treasure they've bought and sold
Another clue awaits you there.
Look around you with great care
At white and black and black and white
Pawn and castle, queen and knight."

I took a great breath. I was feeling a little dizzy.

"Well!" Wanda exclaimed. "That's wacky! Seems like an Otto-style game, if you ask me. He always was up to something to amuse himself."

"Do you—could I—do you think I could have this?"

"It's all yours, darlin'," said Wanda. "Can't see what in the world I would do with it. Now, what is it you came in for?"

"Oh, yeah!" I exclaimed. "I almost forgot. I'm supposed to be picking up glasses for Zack Mack."

"Oh, yes, that good-lookin' boy with all that darlin' hair. Now, where are they? I set them out right here this morning. Oh, here they are. I'll put them in a little bag for you." She put out a hand and clutched my arm. "Bye-bye now, darlin'. I have to get back to work. So thrilled to meet you. Come by any time, and bring your friends."

I stepped out of the store. It seemed like ages since I'd left school. I started running, afraid I'd get into trouble for being gone so long.

fifteen

You see art through your eyes, so your
eyes ought to be a work of art, too.
—Itsuko Furukawa

"So, Willy," Itsuko said, "you want to learn about Giotto."

She smiled. Today she had green eyes again, and they gleamed like a cat's.

She set some large art books on the table in front of us. "Giotto was born in a little town in Italy, the son of a shepherd, in 1267. They say he took care of the flock when he was young and that is why his animals are so especially charming in his paintings. Look at the face on this donkey. Here's Mary and the baby Jesus going off to Egypt." She opened a book and turned to a page that showed a picture.

We all moved close to the book.

"It's so cute!" Gabriela exclaimed. "The donkey is *smiling*."

Itsuko smiled, too. "Giotto caused a change in painting for all time because he painted from nature instead of in the artificial way people had painted before him. Look," she said, holding up the book and turning pages slowly. "His paintings are very clear, with beautiful colors, full of emotion. They are like little scenes, frozen in the moment, showing the drama of the Bible stories. They are painted on the walls of churches, on plaster. They are called frescoes."

"The churches were like these big comic books," Wildman said enthusiastically.

Itsuko raised her eyebrows. "I never thought of it like that. I suppose you are right in a way. Now," she said, "instead of me talking, you look, and tell me what you think."

"This is one mega book," said Zack, picking up one of the largest ones.

"All art books are like that," said Wildman.

"I'm going to be in a book like that someday," said Liesl.

"You're so modest," said Wildman.

"She will be," said Kizzi. "I am sure she will be. She is so good."

"Stop adoring her," said Wildman.

I opened one of the books and began to look. A black-and-white photo of the inside of a church showed how all the scenes were laid out on the walls. Wildman was sort of right—each panel told a chapter in a story.

As I turned the pages of the book I could see what Itsuko meant by the paintings being like little scenes. Here was one with a man standing in front of an iceberg-looking rock, staring down at his feet, maybe because he was sad, or embarrassed, while two shepherds, with all their sheep behind them, stood there, eyeing each other, giving each other this look like they didn't want anything to do with him. They reminded me of Kyle McNulty and Cody Harris, their body language when you got put on their team and they didn't want you. I was glad to see the dog in the painting was at least pawing at the guy in a friendly sort of way.

"Christian stories are a very important part of Italian art," said Itsuko. "Back then, there was no television, no movies, not many books. Most people did not read, so paintings were a way to tell the stories. Giotto was an important storyteller. He is famous for telling the stories of Saint Francis."

"Is there a painting somewhere of Saint Francis and the birds?" I asked.

Itsuko nodded, opening a book and setting it down in front of us. "Here is his famous painting *Saint Francis Preaches to the Birds.*"

There he was—Saint Francis, barefoot, just like Leo had said, in a brown robe, a halo over his head, talking to a flock of birds while another monk stood behind him.

"He can really paint hands!" Liesl said excitedly,

her nose almost touching the page. "The fingers look like real fingers."

"Liesl is right," Itsuko said. "Before Giotto, paintings of people were flat. Giotto made people, and animals, look solid and real and alive."

"I like his halo," said Kizzi. "It's a bright light shining all around his head, and the light is shining out of his head, too."

"I wish I could meet someone like Saint Francis now," said Gabriela. "Someone who treated everyone, animals and birds and insects and people, all the same, and they weren't judging you because of this or that."

"Yeah," said Wildman.

Itsuko cocked her spiked red head to one side. "You know, Saint Francis and his birds, it must be a story people love very much. I saw a lovely little painting of the same subject not that long ago."

I almost jumped out of my skin. "You *did*? *Where*?" The blood was fizzing in my veins again.

"A few months ago I got a call from an antique store," said Itsuko. "Let's see if I can remember the details. I think they said a man just walked in off the street with this little painting. It was obviously quite old, and this man said it had been in his friend's family for a long time, but now the friend wanted to sell it." I sat right up in my chair, hardly able to believe my ears. "The dealers didn't want to buy it until they had it checked out. The whole thing seemed a bit suspicious. They thought it could have been stolen from another antique store or from a museum or from somebody's private collection or something. Well, I did the research for them, and no, it wasn't stolen goods."

Oh, but it was, I wanted to say.

"Did the antique dealers end up buying it?"

Itsuko nodded. "Yes, they gave the man a nice amount for it. And then I approached them about buying it for the gallery. It was such a sweet old painting—quite primitive, but very sweet. I thought it would be a wonderful addition to our collection."

I pushed my chair back and stood up. "Did you?" I looked around wildly, as if expecting to see the painting hanging right here on one of the walls.

Itsuko shook her head. "No, no, they liked it too much. They said they wanted to hang on to it themselves."

"Where is it?" I knew I was practically shouting. "I mean, where are those dealers?"

"What's with you, Willy Wilson?" Liesl asked. Everyone was looking at me strangely.

Itsuko laughed, her cheeks plumping up into two round circles. "I have never seen a boy your age so interested in fine art. Trevor and Cricket Wicklow are the dealers. They own a nice antique store in the West Park. I think it's on Juniper Street. Funny couple. English."

"English!" I repeated.

Go see my friends from England olde. Many a treasure they've bought and sold.

Many a treasure.

Many a *tesoro*?

Was the painting the treasure?

But why have another clue, the chess clue, if it was the treasure? I mean, if the Wicklows had the painting and that was the treasure, then the hunt would be over.

"But it's time for electives now," Itsuko said, looking at her watch. "And I've barely begun talking about the Italian Renaissance. We'll just have to pick this up next time."

"Do you think just for today I could switch from studying famous staircases to the Italian Renaissance," I asked, "so I could go look at that painting?"

Itsuko beamed. "Check with Belle. She's covering the front desk for me right now."

I dashed upstairs. "O-la-la, how marvelous!" Belle exclaimed, clapping her hands when I asked her. "I am thinking how at the Gill Park Gallery School, you, Willy Wilson, you shall learn to love to dig for knowledge, as if for the truffles in the forest."

sixteen

We won't let a piece of furniture go off with
any old wretched soul. We want to make
sure it's going to be well cared for.
—*Trevor and Cricket Wicklow*

"OUT OF MY WAY!" a voice yelled behind me.

I turned and saw Old Violet. She was jetting toward
me on a shopping cart, hanging on to the back of it. I
moved Uncle Roger's bike to the side just in time.

"YAHOO, I GOT WHEELS!" she screeched as she
went by.

I leaned on my bike and stared. She had on about
fifteen coats and a scarf trailed out behind her. It was
amazing the cart even moved as fast as it did with all
those layers she had on.

I rode on, passing the spot where Mitch was building the ice rink. The rink itself was almost done, minus the ice, and work had begun on the rink house. I knew Mitch was pleased by how many people were pitching in and helping in their spare time.

By the time I reached Wicklow Antiques, it was getting dark and cold and it was raining hard. It was great to step inside, where it was warm and dry. The desks and dressers and tables and chests, the sofas and chairs, the china plates and vases, the paintings in their fancy frames, the clocks and lamps—all these things seemed like they were holding their breath waiting for someone to come in and adopt them.

A man sitting at the back of the store behind a glass counter was reading a newspaper.

"Oh dear," he said as he looked up and saw me. "You look like a drowned puppy. Do shake yourself off a bit before you come in any farther, won't you?" he asked. He definitely sounded like he was from *England olde.*

I stood just inside, trying to let the rainwater drip off me, and then as I approached the counter I could see little things displayed on felt trays—jewelry and watches, thimbles, silver spoons. I was supposed to be looking around for *white and black and black and white/Pawn and castle, queen and knight,* but there wasn't anything, so far as I could tell, having to do with chess.

I looked at the man. He had a few dark strands of hair combed across his balding head and a long, bumpy nose. Even though he said, "So, what can we do for you today?" he had gone back to reading his newspaper.

"Do you . . . do you have a painting . . . an old one . . . Italian . . . Saint Francis and the birds?" I asked. I thought I might as well cut right to the chase.

The man's head snapped up. As he took me in, his eyes seemed to grow wider and wider. "CRICKET, CRICKET, COME OUT HERE!" he yelled. "There's another wretched lad come looking for that sweet little painting."

A woman came out from the back of the shop. She was short and a little round, with a head full of brown curls. "What in the world are you caterwauling about this time, Trevor—" She stopped short when she saw me. "Good afternoon," she said. "Or perhaps it's not so good. You look a little drenched, poor thing." She also had an English accent.

"I'm telling you, Cricket, it's another wretched boy looking for Saint Francis and the birds."

Cricket cocked her head to one side, studying me.

"Do you have that painting?" I asked.

"Have had it," said Trevor. He closed up the newspaper and sat with his hands folded on top of the counter.

"Have had it! You mean you sold it!" I said.

"Well, yes," said Trevor.

"Could you . . . um . . . could you tell me who bought it?" I asked.

"The buyer wished to remain anonymous," Cricket explained.

"The buyer comes in and sees the painting," said

Trevor. "He is transported with joy. He says, 'You have a treasure there. I would like to buy that from you.'"

"A treasure," I repeated, feeling prickles up the back of my neck.

"We'd had an expert come look at it," Cricket said. "'It's old,' the expert said. 'And no doubt inspired by the artist Giotto. Our gallery certainly might be interested in it.' But we decided, Trevor and I, that we were rather fond of the thing ourselves and we didn't want to sell it. But then two days later, an art lover comes in, spots the painting, offers us an astonishing sum. We really couldn't turn the offer down."

An astonishing sum. Mr. Pettingill was a rich man. And if he *had* bought the painting, it *could* be the treasure.

"Yes, indeed, an astonishing sum. My darling Cricket and I are going to retire from this wretched business and go live in a château in the Loire valley," said Trevor.

"No, Trevor," said Cricket, sighing, as if they'd been over this a hundred times before. "I keep telling you, *you* can live in France. *I* want a castle in Spain."

"Uh—about the painting?" I just managed to ask.

"Ah, yes . . ." Both Trevor and Cricket turned and looked at me. They didn't say anything at all for a moment.

"A château in the Loire valley," said Trevor again, gazing off into the distance with a dreamy look on his face.

"Can you tell me what the other boy who asked

about it looked like?" I blurted out before Cricket could jump in with her castle in Spain.

"Not an attractive boy," said Cricket thoughtfully. "A ponytail snaking out behind him."

"No, no a thoroughly wretched-looking boy," Trevor agreed. "Although he seemed very anxious about it. It did make me wonder all over again about that fellow who brought it to us in the first place. Something shady about it all, I'm afraid, but it's out of our hands now, in any case."

"About the guy who brought it to you?" I started to ask. "Was he—" Before I could ask whether or not he was in a wheelchair, the door opened. A blast of wet air came in as a man entered, folding up his umbrella.

"Another wretched customer, Cricket," said Trevor. "And it's closing-up time."

"But look who it is," said Cricket in a low voice.

"Oh my, so it is. I guess we'd better curry favor."

I realized with a shock that the man was Roland Brookings, Jr., Mr. Pettingill's once-upon-a-time lawyer—before he got fired.

In the time it took Mr. Brookings to reach Trevor and Cricket, I managed to get myself behind a large chest of drawers. I didn't want him to see me. The last time I had seen him was the night Mr. Brookings lost his chance to buy the park.

"I won't keep you," said Mr. Brookings. My stomach lurched at the sound of his voice, and I suddenly wondered if *he* had been the phony mayor. Maybe that's why the voice had seemed so familiar to me.

"I just came in out of the rain for a moment," he said. "Thought I'd take a look around to see if any new paintings have come in."

"Well, we just got this darling series of Irish portraits you might like to look at," Cricket said.

She trotted out from behind the counter and led him to the opposite corner of the room from where I was standing. I darted for the door.

"Now what's happened to that wretched boy?" Trevor asked. He came out from behind the counter, too. "Oh, there you are, skulking about in the shadows. Do be careful of the furniture, won't you?"

In my rush to escape, I almost toppled over a small table. My hand caught it just in time. My eyes registered that the top of the table was oval-shaped, made up of light and dark squares of wood.

"I consider these to be among the best examples of their kind," Cricket was saying as my brain finally took in the fact that the tabletop was a chess board.

"Lovely piece of nineteenth-century American craftsmanship," Trevor said. He ran his fingers across the squares. "And you see how there's a drawer built right under the top to keep the chess pieces in."

I opened the little drawer, and there, poking out from beneath the black knight, was the edge of what looked like a folded piece of paper.

"I don't think Roland's ever looked at this," Trevor said thoughtfully, turning slightly toward the other side of the room.

My right hand dived for the knight. The fingers of my left hand pounced on the clue.

"Roland, there's a darling little table here I'd like you to see," Trevor called over to Mr. Brookings.

As Cricket and Mr. Brookings approached, I crammed the clue into my pocket and bolted for the door.

"Well, how do you like that," I heard Trevor say as the cold, wet air hit my face. "That wretched boy—"

I stood outside, breathing hard for a moment, letting the rain pelt down. Seeing Roland Brookings, Jr., had made me feel queasy. And Mr. P. had almost blown it. What if Trevor and Cricket had sold the chess table before I had a chance to get to it?

It seemed to rain harder and harder as I rode across the park. It was a cold rain, too, and my hands were freezing.

And then Gill Park music started playing—just three lone notes of a violin. Three chords followed in the same key. It was rich, like hot chocolate. It warmed me up and made me not mind the rain so much.

For the first time in a long time, I thought about playing the violin. Maybe when I got back to Aunt Bridget's and my hands finally warmed up, I'd take out the Hans Zerbe and give it a try.

Just ahead was the toolshed. The roof had a slight overhang, and if I crammed myself against the wall, I could get out of the rain for a moment. There was a utility light, too. I pulled the clue out of my pocket:

Please don't think I'm STRINGing you along.
Honest, Willy, I wouldn't steer you wrong.

But, please now, take careful NOTE.
Even if this poetry's the worst I ever wrote.
You must be SHARP and never FLAT
To find the place the treaure's at.
A zebra may use its hands
To create music for the lands.

Just as I was thinking what an easy clue this was, the door to the toolshed opened, and Zio came out. He stared at me and I stared at him. His face seemed even whiter than usual in the bright light.

"You're Willy," he said.

"Yeah," I said.

"I've been helping Mitch Bloom with the rink house. Finishing up for the day."

"Oh," I said. I stuck the clue back into my pocket.

Zio just stood there. He didn't seem to be in a hurry to go anywhere. "Raining hard," he said. "I remember plenty of nights when I didn't have a roof over my head. That was before I went into the army. In the army I had a bed to sleep in, a roof over my head. Then I fought in a war." His eyes were like two dark wells full of bad memories. "Then I came back here. No home, no place to live. But Old Violet, she found me a place to live."

I nodded, beginning to shiver. "That's good," I said.

"You get on to your home, now," he said. "I'll be seeing you tomorrow at school."

I pushed off on the bike, shoulders hunched against the rain, hoping that wherever Zio was living now, it was okay.

seventeen

If you think it is better to fly than
to swim, you are sadly mistaken.
—*Brother Tortoise*

All the Gill Park Gallery School kids wanted to try out for *The String Man,* so after school on Friday, we all walked across the park to Aunt Bridget's. As we trooped up the stairs I was so excited I thought I was going to explode.

Jack Mack was there. I slapped my hand against my forehead. I had completely forgotten to tell him about Dillon. "Jack, you wouldn't mind if Dillon Deronda showed up to audition, would you?"

"*Dillon?*" Jack looked at me in disbelief. "How in the world did you get Dillon to agree to audition?"

I felt nervous now. "I doubt he'll really come, but I said if he did, we'd pay him."

Everyone in the room was now looking at me as if I'd lost my mind. "When did you talk to Dillon?" Zack asked with interest.

Jack rubbed the top of his smooth head. "Yikes, Willy. I can't pay him! I don't pay kids."

"I doubt he'll even show up," I said.

"Whatever possessed you?" Aunt Bridget asked.

I bent down and scooped Sophie up in my arms. I was embarrassed now. I couldn't begin to explain everything. I hadn't even told any of them I thought the treasure was the Deronda family painting that had been stolen by Dillon's father. I wasn't sure why I was holding back from telling them. Maybe I was waiting until I'd told Dillon himself.

"I thought he'd be good at playing the part of Tazan," I said lamely.

Aunt Bridget was looking thoughtful. "This may be a stroke of genius," she said. "It might be just the thing to keep him off the streets."

"But I can't pay him!" said Jack.

"Well," said Aunt Bridget cheerfully, "let's see if he even shows up. Come on, everybody, let's go."

We rode across town in Jack's van. It was fun, all of us crowded into it, and on the way Jack told us how he had spent half a year converting the space in the old factory into a theater. He had turned it into what he called a black box. It wasn't like a normal stage with curtains. It was an open space with risers where the audience sat, and the stage part was down on the floor, and all the walls were painted black. He had built most of it himself.

When we arrived, a bunch of people, including Gareth, were waiting for Jack outside. I have to admit I was relieved that Dillon wasn't there, even though now I was going to have to go back to his house and try to talk to him about the treasure again.

There were about fifteen kids in all. Jack brought us into the theater through a back door. He made us sit in a circle on the stage area. Then he talked about the play.

"Imagine a jungle, and in the jungle there are two rival villages. They are always at war with each other. Now, in one of the villages twins are born. In this society twins are considered unlucky. The queen of the village arranges to have one of the twins stolen away. This is how the play begins."

He told us about the parts, and then he handed everyone a script. We read bits from the play so we could get a better feeling for it. While we were doing this, Dillon Deronda showed up. He stood at the edge of the room leaning against a wall, slouching, with his hands in his pockets. He was all in black, including a black wool cap, which he wore pulled down almost over his eyes. My heart sank, but Jack paid no attention to him.

After we read some more bits, Jack said, "Okay, I'm going to put you in pairs. Together you'll choose any part of the play that has two people talking. Decide who's going to play whom, and then try to turn it into a scene. Dillon and Zack, you'll work together," he said without even looking at Dillon. "Liesl with Willy, Kizzi with Gabriela . . ." He paired us all up. "Okay, now, everyone get up and go!"

The whole room filled up with noise as everyone started talking at once, hunting through the script to see which part they wanted to try. Liesl was looking sour.

"What's the matter?" I asked.

"It's not like I can really read," she said.

I had forgotten about that.

"Okay," I said. "I'll read a line, and then you repeat it."

"Great," she said, scowling. "Well, anyhow, I want to be the monkey, and she hardly has any lines."

"Yeah, but right now let's do Brother Crow and Brother Tortoise. I'll be the crow, you be the tortoise."

"But I want to be the monkey."

"It's just for right now, Liesl."

We found the part where the two characters were in a bragging contest. I read my lines, and then I fed the lines to Liesl, one at a time. She repeated them after me. The first time through she was slow and stumbled a lot, but very quickly, she remembered, and then she didn't need me to help her. I realized she had an amazing memory.

"Okay, now, get up and try bringing it to life," Jack said. "Everyone up. Nobody should be sitting down. I want you to *move*, and I want you to go through your scene ten times."

"Ten times!" Some kids complained, but then all over the room you could hear bits of the play. The voices got louder and louder as people began to get into what they were doing. Out of the corner of my eye, I could see Dillon and Zack. They were standing up, moving around, speaking the lines.

Liesl tugged on my arm. "Come on, let's do it again."

We tried it again. Liesl had all of the lines down.

Jack Mack stood up and bellowed out in his loudest voice, "All right, now, everyone back in the circle. Sit with your partner, and we'll get started."

The air was full of a kind of nervous, excited energy. Some girls I didn't know were dying to go. It was fun watching them, but nerve-racking, too, waiting. Then it was our turn.

Out of the corner of my eye, I could see Dillon. He was this black blob of bad vibes. He was making me so much more nervous than I would have been without him there.

Then Liesl started doing things she hadn't done when we were just practicing together. I couldn't help reacting to her in ways I hadn't practiced either. At one point she grabbed on to my arm and wouldn't let go. I tried to shake her off. Kids were laughing. When we were done, everyone really clapped, and not just to be polite—everyone, that is, except for Dillon, who looked bored. I didn't care.

Zack and Dillon went next. Dillon got up slowly, acting like he was doing us a big favor. He played Tazan, and he was good. Everyone could feel it. Zack played Imani, the queen of the rival village. At first everyone giggled because he was playing a woman, but then he played it so well, everyone forgot to laugh. When they were finished, everyone clapped loudly again. Dillon sat down without any expression. Zack, you could see, was totally pleased with himself.

Then Jack called on Gabriela and Kizzi. Gabriela spoke right up, with lots of expression, but Kizzi was so quiet you could barely hear her.

Gareth and Wildman were next. Gareth played the String Man and Wildman played Pani, the narrator, who Jack had said could be male or female. Both Gareth and Wildman were clever and funny.

"Okay, great start," Jack said when everyone was done. "I'm not going to cast the play for a while. We'll do this again tomorrow when we meet, and I'll expect you to try different parts. Same time, same place. Put your chairs away, and give me back the scripts."

I saw Dillon leaving, not even bothering to put his chair away. I followed him out of the stage area to the little hallway where we'd first come in.

eighteen

One time when I was a little boy, I wanted the
fire truck the kid across the street had. I
screamed for two days until they all gave up
and finally gave it to me.

—*Frank Featherstone*

"Dillon!"

"Oh, Shark Bait, it's you," Dillon said. High up on
the wall there were a couple of windows. The light
coming in was eerie, creating weird shadows under
his eyes.

"Listen, Dillon, about the treasure."

"Forget it, will you? I'm not interested in baby
treasure hunts."

Some kids walked by and pushed out the door. Cold air rushed in.

"How about old paintings? Are you interested in those?"

Dillon blinked hard. His eyebrows raised up a millimeter. You could see his jaw muscles working. More kids walked by.

"I'm beginning to think the treasure is your family's painting," I said.

"How do you know about that?"

"Your grandparents told me."

Dillon's face darkened, and then he swore as he kicked a wall. "What business is it of yours?"

"The park is my business."

Dillon yanked off his hat. "How do I know this isn't some big scam of yours?" he asked, twisting the hat in his hands.

I pulled out the small piece of paper that had been wadded up in my pocket. "I have a clue here. It says the treasure is a work of art. And it sent me to the antique store where your dad sold it, or got a friend of his to sell it for him." Dillon tried to grab the clue from me, but for once I was too quick for him. I read it out loud.

"And it wasn't there, was it?" he asked.

I remembered that Dillon had probably been to Wicklow Antiques. "No, but that's the whole point. They said someone bought it for a lot of money. I'm almost sure it was Mr. Pettingill."

Aunt Bridget came in. "Oh, there you are. We've

been looking for you," she said. "Hi, Dillon," she added brightly. "You were great in that part!"

Dillon grunted slightly.

"We're leaving, Willy," she said. "We'll be in the van waiting for you."

The others streamed by—Jack, Zack, Gareth, all the other Gallery School kids.

"I'll be there in a second," I said.

When they were gone, Dillon started pacing back and forth. "There's just one problem with your little treasure hunt," he said.

"What's that?" I said.

"Another dude claims he has the painting." He leaned against a wall and folded his arms across his chest.

"Another dude?"

"Ever heard of a guy named Frank Featherstone?"

I could feel my throat closing up. I thought of the black limousine that had pulled up in Dillon's neighborhood.

"I made a deal with him," Dillon said. He paused for a long moment. "The deal is I wreck the park so that it gets taken away from you. And when that happens, he gives me back the painting."

I felt as if he'd kicked me in the stomach.

"That Blue Gang stuff—it's all his idea. That stupid getup, spray painting Mitch Bloom's tree." Dillon jammed the hat back on his head.

My insides started swirling.

Maybe it had been Frank Featherstone who bought the painting from Trevor and Cricket, not Mr. Pettingill. Then another thought hit me—the way Roland Brookings, Jr., had been so buddy-buddy with the Wicklows. He could have bought it. Or he and Featherstone could have bought it together, the way they'd tried to buy the park together.

Dillon stretched and yawned, and then in a bored tone of voice, he said, "So I don't know what your little treasure hunt is all about, but it's not about my family's painting."

I swallowed hard, trying to think clearly. "You've actually seen the painting? You know he has it?"

Dillon blinked, and didn't say anything for a moment. "No," he finally said in a slightly strangled voice.

I couldn't believe it. "You took his *word* for it?"

"Yeah," he muttered. "He described it. In detail. I don't know how he could have done that unless he had it."

My insides began to settle down. I swallowed hard. "Well, being able to describe it doesn't mean he has it."

Dillon stood still without saying anything, but I felt new energy pouring into my veins.

"Look, Dillon, it all adds up. Who are you going to believe? Mr. Pettingill or that jerk?"

Dillon shrugged, his face closed up into its usual bored expression. "I'll let you know," he said. He touched two fingers to his forehead, pushed out the door, and was gone before I could say another word.

Inside the van the windows were all steamed up. I sat way in the back, next to Gareth.

"What part am I going to get?" Liesl asked. She was sitting just behind Jack, so she could whine into his right ear.

"Time will tell," said Jack.

"I want to be the monkey," said Liesl.

"I know," Jack grunted.

"Can I be the monkey?" Liesl asked, her voice getting higher and whinier.

Gareth poked me with his elbow, and we looked at each other and grinned.

Jack dropped off Gabriela and Fernando, and then Kizzi. As soon as they were gone, Wildman said, "Yo, I was playing Black Avenger last night, and man, I had definite pawnage." He turned around in his seat to talk to Gareth and me, and he didn't stop until Jack pulled the van up in front of his apartment building.

"We're here, Wildman," said Jack.

"Hey, man, thanks for the ride," said Wildman as he climbed out. "And I really like the play."

After he left, it was so quiet in the van it made my ears hurt.

"Wow," said Gareth. "That guy sure can talk."

"Call Mitch on your cell phone, Liesl, so he'll know to meet you at the edge of the woods, and move up, Gareth and Willy," said Aunt Bridget. "I want to be able to talk to you. What was the big meeting with Dillon, Willy?"

I waited for Liesl to get off the phone, and then I

blurted out, "I think I found out what the treasure is in Mr. P.'s treasure hunt." I was so happy, finally to be sharing things. "And it turns out that it's something Dillon is looking for, too."

And then I told them the whole story of the painting by Dillon's ancestor, and about finding the clues, and how Itsuko Furukawa at the school had been asked to look at the painting. I told them what had happened at Trevor and Cricket Wicklow's, and finally, what Dillon had just told me about Frank Featherstone.

"You should tell this story to my dad," said Gareth. "And he'll tell the mayor."

"Even if you tell the real mayor, there's no proof," said Jack. "Featherstone'll just deny it."

"So, who really has the painting?" Aunt Bridget asked.

"I don't know," I said. "But I'm hoping the treasure hunt will lead us to it. Dillon hasn't actually seen the painting, you know. Featherstone just *says* he has it. What's bothering me is that he described it perfectly to Dillon. And how did he even know about it in the first place?"

There was silence in the van as we all thought about this.

"So, what do you think Dillon will do?" Aunt Bridget asked finally.

"I don't know," I said. "He wants that painting, that's for sure."

"And he wants that part, that's for sure," Jack added.

"How do you know?" Zack asked.

"Well, for one thing, he took the script home with him," Jack said. "But even without that, I can usually tell when a kid is hooked. I'd say you were hooked, aren't you, Liesl?"

"Does that mean you're giving me the part?" Liesl asked.

"Off you go, you cute little mongoose, you," Jack said with a laugh. We had reached the edge of the park closest to the woods. Jack pulled up to the curb. "This is where the bus stops. And there's Mitch waiting for you."

"Think about me for the part of the monkey," she yelled into the van just before she shut the door.

After Jack dropped Aunt Bridget and me off in front of our apartment, I stood in the street breathing in the cold air. I could see the moon, full and bright, stuck right in between two buildings.

Who had bought the painting? Mr. Pettingill? Brookings? Featherstone?

The craggy face in the moon stared down at me. It seemed to be smiling, and the smile seemed familiar. It seemed to me as if good old Mr. P. had become the man-in-the-moon just so he could look down on me and keep an eye on things.

nineteen

When I throw my knuckleball, I like watching
kids turn into pretzels when they try to hit it.
—*Dillon Deronda*

The next day at school Mr. Kim said he was going to
take us to one of the labs at Gloria University so we
could look through their powerful microscopes.

"There is so much in the universe we can't see,"
he said. "How amazing that everything"—his head
bobbed up out of his collared shirt and he spread his
arms wide—"is made up of these things that we can't
see. Do you know there are scientists who believe
that the tiniest particles of all are tiny, extremely thin,
almost rubber-band-like strands they call strings?"

"Strings?" We all looked at him like he'd lost his mind.

"Any connection to *The String Man*?" Wildman asked Zack. "Seems like everyone's talking about string these days."

"When we get there, Liesl," said Mr. Kim, "you will work with Wildman. William will work with Gabriela, Kizzi with Zackary. It's good you're here, William. Now we have even numbers."

"I don't want to work with that geek," Liesl muttered under her breath.

"What is the derivation of the word *geek,* Liesl?" Mr. Kim asked.

"What does *deriv*-whatever mean?" asked Liesl.

"Find that out, too," said Mr. Kim.

"You ask a question around here, and he answers with a question," Liesl said to me. "It's the hemlock guy's style of teaching."

"What hemlock guy?" I asked.

"Socrates. Mr. Kim told us about him. He was an Ancient Geek," said Liesl with a grin.

"Oh," I said.

"*O,*" repeated Mr. Kim. "The fifteenth letter of the alphabet." Everyone groaned. "Derived from the Phoenician alphabet as omicron. It is used in the alphabets of all western European languages. In the word *amoeba,* the *O* is silent."

I had to admit, in spite of myself, that almost every time Mr. Kim opened his mouth, I could feel my brain sparking up.

"Now we're going to hop on the number six bus

and go across town to the university," he said. "Every-one ready? And I don't need to mention that getting to use the university lab is a very great privilege."

That night we all rode in Jack's van to the theater again. The rehearsal began with a warm-up. Just as before, Dillon came slinking in, all in black again, and stood against the wall watching the activity.

"All right," said Jack. "I'm pairing everyone up again. Different partners. And make sure you choose a different character to work on."

I couldn't believe it. Jack put me with Dillon. Dillon rolled his eyes.

"Okay," he said, stepping up to me. "We'll do the scene where Tazan talks to Etak. I'll be Tazan and you be Etak."

"But Jack said we couldn't play the same parts as yesterday," I said. "And Etak is a girl."

"I don't care what he said, and who cares if she is a girl? Zack played Imani yesterday, and he didn't say, 'Eww, I'm not playing a girl.'" Dillon pulled the script out of his back pocket.

We started working on the scene, but I didn't like working with Dillon. He made me too nervous.

"Put a little life into it," Dillon complained. "Etak is supposed to stand up to her father."

I was relieved when Jack finally called us into the circle. Gabriela and Wildman were working together today, and they went first. They were both just as good as they had been the day before. Then Jack called on Dillon and me.

Everyone clapped, but Jack looked serious. "You're very good in that part, Dillon. But I said to try a different role from yesterday, so you and Willy need to go into that back room over there and prepare a different scene." He nodded in the direction of a door.

There was this awkward silence. At first I didn't think Dillon would go. He squinted his ratty eyes, and you could see his jaw muscles working away. But then he turned to me and said, "Let's go."

We went through the door into the back room. There was an old couch in it and a few chairs. I sat down, but Dillon remained standing. "You choose something," he said. "I don't care what."

I cleared my throat nervously. "What about the treasure hunt?" I asked. "Did you make a decision?"

"Maybe," he said, looking straight ahead.

"Well?"

"Just find a part, will you?"

I started turning the pages of the script without really seeing the words. Dillon made me so mad everything was blurry.

"We'll do the crow and tortoise scene," he said. "You be the tortoise. You'll be good at being slow."

So much for letting me choose the part. We practiced it a few times, Dillon acting like a robot. He didn't put any expression at all into what he was saying.

When we went out to the stage, Kizzi was performing with Gareth. Gareth was playing Eridemius, the poet/slave. Kizzi was doing the part of Aerisone, the older sister, but she giggled every time Gareth said his lines. She wasn't exactly the bossy older sister type.

Jack had a few other people go, and then it was our turn again. Dillon was actually surprisingly funny, and everyone laughed at him, but I felt like I was a stick of wood, barely able to push words out of my mouth.

As I sat down I made a decision about Dillon. I wasn't going to let him in on the treasure hunt, even if he got down on his hands and knees and begged me.

The rehearsal was over. Jack caught Dillon as we were getting up. "Put your chair away," he said. "And I don't mind if you keep the script, but ask me first."

Dillon blinked and then cocked his head to one side. "Do you *mind*," he asked, extra-polite, "if I take this script with me?"

"No, I don't mind at all," said Jack, not losing his cool. "In fact, I think it's terrific. But I'm going to tell you something else, Dillon." He folded his arms across his chest and looked directly at Dillon. "I'm not paying you. I know Willy said something about you being paid, but I don't pay kids." He let Dillon take that in, and then he went on. "And don't count on getting the part of Tazan. So now you might not want to be in the play at all, but I hope you do. I think you've got talent, and I would enjoy working with you."

Jack turned and walked out of the room without saying another word.

Dillon muttered under his breath as he folded up his chair.

I took a deep breath and spoke up. "I've decided I'm not doing the treasure hunt with you even if you decide you want to." My legs were a little shaky, and my mouth felt dry. "I feel like I never know where you're coming from," I said, avoiding Dillon's eyes. "I don't think it would work."

"He doesn't have the painting." Dillon's voice came out like a croak. "I met him and told him I wanted to see it. I said I wouldn't do anything else to the park until I saw it with my own eyes. He said he had it in safekeeping somewhere, so he couldn't show it to me. I know he was lying."

Just then Jack came back into the room.

"Get the lights, and let's boogie on out of here," he said.

I found a row of light switches on the wall.

"Just hit all of them," said Jack.

Click, click, click, all the lights went out. Dillon and I followed Jack out, and then we were standing outside in the cold parking lot.

"I'll meet you tomorrow after school," Dillon said in a rushed sort of way.

"Okay," I said, and then he was gone.

I looked up at Mr. P.-in-the-moon. "What I want to know is did you plan this?" I asked him out loud. "Did you know all along the painting belonged to Dillon? Was this some big scheme of yours to make us work together?"

"Willy's losing his mind," Liesl yelled out the window. "He's talking to the moon!" I climbed into the van.

"So," Liesl started in. "What about the monkey? Have you decided the parts yet, Jack?"

twenty

Not every tree can be a violin,

not every dog a spaniel.

—Hans Zerbe

We were so busy at school I didn't have time to think about Dillon until it was actually time to meet him.

He stood outside the gallery, hands crammed into his pockets, black hat pulled halfway down over his eyes. The guy never seemed to wear very much. Maybe he never got cold. He had ice in his veins instead of blood.

Liesl came out the gallery door and ran down the steps. She gave me a look as she went by, head tossed in the air. We had had a fight earlier. I had said she couldn't come with us.

Zio came out next and stopped when he saw Dillon. He came over and loomed his white face right into Dillon's. "It's time for you to shape up, wise guy. I know what you've been up to."

Dillon's hands came right up against Zio's big chest.

"I said *wise up*." Zio glared for a few more seconds and then backed off, turned on his heels, and walked away.

For a moment I thought Dillon was going to go after him, but then he just swallowed hard and shrugged.

"That was Zio, our guard. He seemed to know you."

"I know who he is," said Dillon. "My uncle Gino and I work with him sometimes with Mitch Bloom. He's a real moron." He turned to me. "So, Shark Bait—"

"My name is Willy," I said. My fingers clenched the clue, even though I knew it by heart now.

Dillon grinned. "Just kidding," he said. "Go on, Willy, read it to me."

"I already know what it is," I said when I had finished reading. "It's the violin maker, Hans Zerbe."

"Oh, a violin maker," Dillon drawled. He rolled his eyes.

"You don't have to come."

"I do have to come. Unfortunately. So let's go."

We crossed the street and went into the park. It was almost dark now, and the streetlamps were on.

"So where does this Hans Zerbe dude live?" he asked.

"In the West Park, on Short Street. It's supposed to be off Pearl Street."

"So what do we say when we get there? He's not going to believe I'm interested in violins."

I couldn't help smiling. "I sort of thought about that," I said. "Mr. Pettingill actually gave me a Hans Zerbe violin—"

"He would," Dillon cut in bitterly. "A park wasn't enough."

"Look, it's not like owning the park is making me rich or anything. It's a big worry. And basically, it's my fault if it gets wrecked."

"Yeah, well."

We walked up and down Pearl Street a few times but didn't see a Short Street. We stopped and asked people. No one had heard of it.

Dillon was getting impatient. "Let's give it up," he said. "It's probably on the other side of the park or something, or maybe you got it wrong and it's really Long Street."

Just then I saw Jerry Rabinowitz come out of a little dark alley we had passed a couple of times. Jerry was a poet who hung out in the park all the time, but I hadn't seen him since last summer. Every poem he wrote had to have the word *green* in it, so I guessed maybe he liked the park better when it wasn't winter.

"Hey, Willy Wilson," he said, coming up to me. "Long time no see. How's life been treatin' ya?"

"Well," I said, "I've been worried about the park."

"Yeah," he grunted. "That Blue Gang. The least they could do is use green if they're going to go around coloring things. Then I'd have something to write about."

I glanced at Dillon, barely able to keep the grin off my face. He was looking down at his feet, scowling.

"Say, Jerry, do you know where Short Street is?"

Jerry jerked his thumb back at the alley. "Right behind you," he said.

I peered down it. "It's short, all right."

"*Green graffiti, ivy made of alphabets, grows gregariously when gangs grope in the dark of night.* How's that for a first line? Good to see ya, Willy. You inspired me!"

We stared after Jerry as he bounded away, and then we turned down Short Street. It was paved with cobblestones, and all the houses had signs on them saying they were historic. At the end of the street, there was an old-fashioned-looking streetlamp. In the light we could see a sign hanging over the door of the last house. The sign had a painting of a violin on it, and it read HANS ZERBE, LUTHIER.

I reached out and pressed the doorbell. We waited, and when no one came to the door, I pressed it again. As a window opened above us classical music came pouring out, and then a man's head poked out. "Just a minute," the man shouted. "I'm in my shop."

The window shut, and in a moment an outside light came on as the door opened. Out stepped a short man with a head of thick gray hair and a full gray beard. He peered at us, the heads of three cocker spaniels peeking out from behind his legs. "Yes, hallo, can I help you?" The dogs were yapping. "Clara! Franz! Volfgang!" he called to them. The dogs stopped yapping. He peered at us again. "That's better. Can I help you?"

"I'm . . . I'm Willy Wilson. I wanted to meet you. Mr. Pettingill left me one of your violins."

"Ahh, yah, I know who you are," he said, reaching out and shaking my hand. "Come in, come in. I am pleased to meet you." He stepped back from the door. "Clara, Franz, Volfgang!" he called to the dogs again. "Let these boys come in. Otto Pettingill," he went on as he led us through a hallway, "he was my good friend. It is because of him I came to Gloria in the first place. He held a contest, a long time ago now, for the best violin made from scratch—that is, from the very beginning, from a tree! I came all the way from Germany to enter the contest. And my violin, she won me the first prize, a large sum of money in those days. I liked Gloria so much I stayed, and then I married, and then I had four children. Then my lovely wife passed on and the children all grew up and moved away, but still I am here in Gloria, all because of Herr Pettingill."

We were in the living room now. The walls were lined with bookcases and paintings that could have been in the gallery. A grand piano took up half the room, a music stand beside it, a violin case resting on top. Dillon stood uncomfortably on the Oriental carpet.

"So," said Hans, "you are Villy Vilson, and you are. . . ?" He turned to Dillon, and then his whole face lit up. "Och, but I know who you are. You are that boy, that pitcher, for the team—what is it?—Sharks, that's it!"

Dillon looked at him in disbelief. "You know who I am?"

Hans clapped Dillon on the shoulder. "Do I know who you are? Listen, my friend, I have a very great veakness. I love American baseball! Come, come, I show you."

We followed him up several flights of stairs. The spaniels wriggled up with us, their nails clicking on the stairs. We passed more paintings on the walls. Finally, on the fourth floor, we walked through a room to the end where there was a glass door. Hans slid it open and turned on some lights.

"Come," he said. We were outside now, on a deck. He pointed to a large telescope. "You can't see so good right now, but here is a view of the park. I watch all the games. I watch you, Dillon Deronda, since you were this high." He held his hand about level with Dillon's knees. "That last game against the Gorillas was a tough one." He shook his head. "But you going places, my friend," he said to Dillon. He shivered a little. "It's not summertime out here. We go back inside."

We stepped back in, Hans sliding the door shut and turning off the outside lights. We, and the dogs, followed him back down all the flights of stairs to his living room. Dillon seemed to breathe more easily. He even leaned down and patted the dogs.

"So," Hans said, turning to me, "you have one of my violins, a gift from my old friend Otto. You like it?"

"I . . . to tell you the truth, I think it's too good for me."

"Ach! So you do not play it?"

"Only a little," I lied. I hadn't played it at all. Aunt Bridget hadn't found me a teacher yet, either.

Hans stared at me, stroking his beard. "You come with me. Clara, Franz, Volfgang, *kommen zie hier*!"

He motioned for us to follow him again. This time we went up only one flight of stairs.

"Keep looking for the clue," I muttered to Dillon.

"No! Really?" he asked sarcastically.

twenty-one

People always want to know how I keep my nerve when I'm pitching under pressure. It's pretty simple. I just pretend all the batters are penguins, and they can't hit and they can't run.
—*Waldo Yadzinski*

"Here is my vorkshop, my pride, my joy," said Hans. He opened a door and stepped into a room, the dogs scrambling in ahead of him. They headed for a corner, grunting and groaning as they lay down. "It smells good, yah?" he asked. "Wood, oil, varnish—like a good soup."

As I looked around, I saw rows of chisels and gouges lined up in neat slots along the back of a workbench, and hanging above it, little hand planes, sharp knives, and a whole lot of clamps. Above another bench hung violin-shaped paper patterns. One shelf was filled with small glass jars. "Varnish," Hans said, following my glance. "The way the violin looks in the end, it all depends on the varnish." Another shelf was filled with china spaniels.

A high stool was pulled up close to the workbench, little curls of wood lying in a heap below it. A bright lamp shone on a thin piece of wood that looked liked the top of a violin, a chisel next to it.

"Now then," he said to me, "you shut your eyes."

"Shut my eyes?"

"Shut your eyes."

Feeling ridiculous, I shut my eyes. I heard the sound of a violin case being opened, and then a violin being tuned.

"Here you go." He pressed a violin into my hands. "Keep your eyes shut, but don't drop it, yah?" Next, he handed me a bow. "Now, you play, but keep your eyes shut."

I tucked the violin under my chin, arched my left hand into position, held the bow with my right. "I haven't played in a long time," I said. "And with my eyes shut—"

"Take your time, take your time."

I played a scale, first up and then down, my fingers automatically finding the right places. I was glad my old violin teacher had made me practice scales a lot.

"Oww, my ears," Dillon said in a fake whiny voice.

"Pay no attention to him," said Hans. "He plays baseball, not violins. The only music he knows is the roar of the crowd. But okay, enough with the scale. Now play. You can do it. Play something you know well."

Even if my eyes had been open, I sure didn't want to play something *he* knew well. So I decided to play the park song I had made up at the end of last summer. I had been looking at the fountain from Aunt Bridget's apartment, watching the colors change, when this tune came into my head. Then I added chords that seemed to match kids skateboarding and Gareth yelling at kids while he was coaching baseball, and I plucked the strings to make the ping of the bat. I even had a bunch of minor chords, which were dark and a little sour, like Dillon.

When I finished, I heard one pair of hands clapping.

"Can I open my eyes now?"

Hans Zerbe laughed. "Och, yah, open your eyes. You pretty good with your eyes shut. You know that piece well. Nice little melody. What is it?"

"It's something I made up." I looked at the violin I had been playing. It was a mix of honey and gold.

"You made it up!" Hans exclaimed. "We have a budding composer on our hands." He looked at me, stroking his beard. "Maybe you not the player, but the poet. Think about that one. Bye the bye, that's a Stradivarius you been plucking."

I was so startled I almost dropped the violin.

"Don't worry if you drop it. It's only worth a few million!"

I cringed, handing both violin and bow back to him as quickly as I could.

"A Hans Zerbe violin is too good to play, but you waltz no problem on the Strad!" said Hans. "I am flattered. This Strad, she was made in Italy about five hundred years ago."

Five hundred years and from Italy!

"Not as old as the painting," I said to Dillon, "but still—" Dillon nodded, his eyes glued to the violin.

"Five hundred years," Hans went on, as if he hadn't heard. "And I am part of that history," he said proudly. "I carry on the tradition. The only difference is I use a band saw," he said, pointing to where it stood across the room, "and, oh yes, the electric grinder for sharpening my tools. And five hundred years ago they didn't have sandpaper. They used sharkskin!" He opened his eyes wide, looking serious for a moment. "You act afraid, and the violin, like an animal, she knows. You need to attack with bravura, like Dillon on the pitcher's mound. Be excited, *so*!"

He tucked the violin under his chin and began to play. The instrument jumped alive in his hands. His eyes were half-closed, his mouth in a half-smile, as his whole body moved with the bow.

Dillon watched with a look of amazement.

"How'd you learn to play like that?" Dillon asked when Hans finished.

Hans shrugged. "I practice," he said as he put the violin carefully back into a case that was on a table behind him. "I teach my fingers. I trust my fingers. Just like a pitcher when he throws a knuckleball, yah?" He turned to Dillon. "And I just am thinking, I got something for you."

"For me?" Dillon looked startled.

"Yah, yah, for you. Villy, he gets a violin, so you should get something, too. I got just the thing. I'll be back in a minute. Don't go to Chicago or anything while I'm away." He chuckled to himself as he left the room, the spaniels panting after him.

Dillon and I looked at each other. Dillon was actually grinning.

"We ought to be looking around for the clue," I said.

"I already got it," he said.

"What?"

"While you were sawing away on that old hunk of wood with your eyes shut, I nabbed it."

"Where was it?"

Dillon pointed to the row of little china spaniels. "One of them was wearing a collar." He pulled a small, folded-up piece of paper out of his pocket.

"Have you read it yet?" I asked.

"Yeah," he said.

"Well?"

"Wouldn't you like to know?" He held it up in front of me, a ratty smile on his face.

I would have lunged at him, but Hans and the dogs came back into the room. Hans was carrying a baseball glove. "Take a look at this baby." He handed the glove to Dillon. "I bought it at an auction."

Dillon turned it over in his hands. "It says Waldo Yadzinski," he said in amazement. "This is Waldo Yadzinski's glove? The great *Yad*?"

"Well, happy birthday," said Hans.

Dillon stared at Hans in disbelief. *"You're giving me the Yad's glove?"*

"Yah, who else better to give it to? Put it on, put it on!"

"It fits," said Dillon.

"Yah, it fits like a glove," said Hans with a smile.

"Thank you," said Dillon.

"Yah, it's my pleasure," said Hans, clapping his hand on Dillon's shoulder again. "You remember me when you make it big. You send me tickets to a game."

"I will," said Dillon.

"Got to get to work now, boys. You come back and visit, though."

He walked with us down the stairs and toward the door. Clara, Franz, and Wolfgang came with us, too. Dillon kept the glove on his left hand.

"You, Villy," Hans said to me. "You play my violin. You hurt her feelings keeping her locked up all day and night."

I nodded. I thought it would be much easier now.

Dillon and I headed back up the short Short Street and turned onto Pearl. Neither of us said anything. I didn't feel like talking to Dillon. Maybe I never would again. He was too hard to deal with.

"Hey," said Dillon. He stopped walking. In spite of myself, I stopped walking, too. He dug his right hand into his pocket and brought up the clue. "Here," he said, holding it out to me.

twenty-two

Setting up clues for a treasure hunt makes
you think about all the things that are
most important in your life.
—*Otto Pettingill*

I read the clue out loud:

> *"Because not just royalty wears a crown*
> *He helps the homeless not to frown.*
> *His work is difficult, it takes skill—*
> *A craftsman, he must fill and drill.*
> *A craftsman like the painter who*
> *So long ago sat there and drew*
> *What now is treasure that you seek.*
> *I hope you find it by next week."*

"A dentist?" I wondered out loud.

"No, duh," said Dillon.

"Well, there must be a few thousand dentists in this town," I said, trying to ignore him. "But the way the other clues have gone, there's a good chance he was Mr. Pettingill's dentist."

"How do we know who his stupid dentist was?" Dillon asked.

I tried to think. "Maybe Liesl goes to the same dentist, since Mr. P. was her guardian for all those years."

"Couldn't be a very good dentist. I always thought she had crummy-looking teeth," said Dillon.

"Or Belle Vera might know, since she took care of Liesl. I can ask them both at school, and I'll tell you at rehearsal," I said. "If you do the play," I added.

Dillon punched his right fist into his new glove. "Yeah, I don't know. It depends on what part I get."

"He practically comes right out and says the treasure is the painting," I said.

"Yeah," said Dillon. Then he touched his fingers to his hat and said, "Well, see ya. If you find out the name, you can call my grandparents and leave a message."

The first thing I did when I got home was take out the violin. I pictured Hans Zerbe sitting on his stool in his workshop carving it. I held it up, admiring the way it curved just so, and pressed it against my face. It was so smooth.

Then I tuned it up, and just for fun I played like Hans Zerbe, wildly pulling the bow across the strings.

There was clapping behind me. I turned around and saw Aunt Bridget in the doorway.

"That was interesting," she said.

I burst out laughing.

"It's good to hear you playing again," she said. "I think."

At school the next day I asked Liesl during a break between classes who her dentist was.

"Dentist?" she asked blankly.

"You know, someone who takes care of your teeth?"

Liesl frowned, looking thoughtful. It was Friday, a cool day, and she was wearing a soccer jersey and a sort of lacy black skirt over a pair of red tights, with red high-tops on her feet.

"Some woman Belle Vera goes to."

"A woman? Are you sure?"

"Of course I'm sure. They're my teeth, aren't they?"

The clue referred to a "he." I didn't think Liesl's dentist could be the right one.

I spent the next hour watching Mr. Kim put red marks all over an essay I had written. "Over the weekend I expect you to rewrite the paper, and I expect to see some actual thinking," he said.

I slumped away with my marked-up essay and found Belle downstairs, sitting at the front counter. I asked her if she knew who Mr. Pettingill's dentist was.

"Den-tiste?" she asked, looking at me in surprise. "You ask me who was his den-tiste?" She shook her head. "Perhaps at one time I knew this, but now, let me think. It was a name that amuses, but what was it?" She muttered to herself. "I am thinking it begins with the letter *V*?"

I was glad Mr. Kim wasn't standing right there. *"The letter* V . . ." I could almost hear him saying.

I grabbed the phone book, which was stacked on a desk behind the counter, and started looking in the Yellow Pages under DENTISTS. There were, as I had thought, a ton of dentists in Gloria. Belle and I looked through the *V*'s.

"No," she said, shaking her head. "Nothing is ringing the bell. But I shall reflect."

Liesl came up the stairs from the ground floor. "I GOT THE PART! I GOT THE PART! I GOT THE PART!" she screeched. "I'm Sister Monkey!"

"How do you know?" I asked.

"Jack Mack posted it on the Net, and Wildman saw it and told me."

Wildman came up next, holding the list in his hand, Kizzi and Gabriela behind him. "I'm Tazan," he said, his voice full of surprise. "I totally didn't expect it. Dillon is Brother Crow."

"Dillon is Brother Crow? Who am I?" I asked, suddenly too nervous to look at the list for myself.

"Brother Tortoise," Wildman said with a grin. "You'll be perfect."

I took a breath. I hadn't expected to get such a big part. I thought for sure I'd be a villager or something. "Let me see the list," I said.

Lots of the kids who had turned up for the audition were villagers, Fernando among them. A girl named Ellen was Pani; a girl named Sarah was playing

Imani; Gabriela was Aerisone, the older sister. Kizzi and a girl named Marnie, who was tall like Kizzi, were the twin sisters.

"Wow, Kizzi," I said. "That's a good part."

"I hope I can handle it," she said, looking scared.

"You can handle it," said Gabriela. "I'll be on stage with you a lot, and I can help you."

No surprise—Gareth was the String Man. What *was* a surprise was that Zack was playing the poet/slave. He came up just then, and we told him what part he had. He ran his fingers through his curly hair.

"I know," he said. "Dad told me. I thought for sure I'd be one of the animals. This is kind of a serious part for me, but Bridget said I should play it because it would bring out my sensitive side. And I guess Bridget is bringing out Dad's more sensitive side because he's doing what she suggested." He grinned.

We were all sure that Dillon would quit the play, but he showed up at the last possible minute, making a point of not looking at, or speaking to, anyone.

The first thing Jack did was hand out the scripts that were now going to be ours for good. Then he gave us a pep talk about how excited he was, and how great we were going to be, and how we had to be sure to set aside time for memorizing, since we had only about a month to get it down. Finally, he said how important it was for us to come to the rehearsals. Then he divided us up into groups based on what scenes we were in. I was with Dillon and

Liesl, and Aunt Bridget was going to be working with us to begin with.

"Found out who the dentist is yet?" Dillon asked. I shook my head. He looked at Liesl. "Does she know?" I shook my head again.

"Okay," said Aunt Bridget, coming over to us. "First things first. Liesl has to learn how to swing in on a rope. I'm sure you guys won't object to a little swinging yourself."

The next hour and a half was about the most fun I'd ever had in my life. We launched off a ladder holding on to a thick rope that was attached by a cable to the ceiling. Wrapping hands and feet around the rope, we went flying out across the stage. We practiced that for a while, and then we got down to the actual speaking parts.

Brother Crow and Brother Tortoise spend most of the play bragging to each other about who is better and why. As we practiced, Aunt Bridget kept laughing. "You guys are so naturally prickly with each other it's a riot," she said.

"I'm glad *you* think it's a riot," I said.

Liesl was just plain funny as Sister Monkey. At one point Dillon and I had to lunge at each other and roll on the floor, and then Liesl would jump on top of both of us. She didn't have any trouble at all doing that.

At the end of the rehearsal, I was sore all over, but happy. I was so excited to be in a play.

twenty-three

My first job was in a shoe store. All those
shoelaces! All those smelly feet! If it hadn't
been for Otto Pettingill, I might have just
stayed selling shoes all my life. He believed
in me way back when no one else did.

—Merla

A couple of weeks later, we spent one whole evening
rehearsal working on the scenery. And what a surprise to find out that the artist Jack had hired to
work with us was Merla. I couldn't wait to see if she
looked like her self-portrait.

Merla had a loft on the top floor of the Art Factory, and to get to it, we had to come in through the

lobby. Liesl's mural was there, half-finished. I realized as I stood and looked at it that it was a bigger and slightly different version of a picture she had given me at the end of the summer.

It showed Mr. Pettingill inside a room playing the piano, with notes swirling around his head and then floating out the window into the park. Then the notes mixed with the water gushing out of the fountain and blended in with Colonel Pettingill riding his horse or flew into Jerry Rabinowitz's ears as he sat on a bench writing poetry. Just like in my picture, she squeezed a whole bunch of things in: the Gorillas and Sharks playing baseball, the tree house, and Mitch's garden. In this one she had added the skating rink and the rink house and the brick oven.

It was also on a much bigger scale than the one she had given me. I didn't know how such a small person had managed to fill all that space.

"Come on." Liesl nudged me with a sharp, bony elbow. "Let's go."

On the way up to the top floor, I kept getting sidetracked, checking out the long hallways, each with rooms off them. All kinds of classes were going on, like tai chi and karate, ceramics and printing. The stairs and the floors creaked like crazy, especially with the whole cast of *The String Man* going up them.

When Merla came to the door, I was surprised because in her self-portrait she had long red hair, and now it was short and blonde, but her expression was just as fierce. I think it was the way her red eyebrows came down like lightning bolts toward her nose, with deep lines between them like she spent a lot of time thinking. But otherwise, she was kidlike in a white T-shirt and paint-stained overalls.

"Come on in," she said, motioning for us to step into the huge room behind her. It had a wooden floor and big windows and lots of wall space. Large wooden frames with some sort of white canvasy-looking fabric stretched across them—I learned later they were called scenery flats—stood everywhere. We could see the shoe of someone who was working behind them, and then a hand poked out as it held the frame, and there was a loud shooting sound of a staple gun.

"Howdy, Jack, we're ready for you, at least we're almost ready for you," Merla said, nodding at the flats. "I've been a little ditzy lately, maybe because I dyed my hair blonde. I didn't think of that before. Maybe *that's* the problem, but I'm pretty sure it's because of this tea I've been drinking. It's supposed to have this herb in it that improves your memory, but it turned out that this herbal tea has little doses of *arsenic* in it—like arsenic is *poison*, you know. Well, I cut that out because I've got this exhibition coming up—a big show, my latest work. It's called Art as Sport or Sport as Art, or SPART. The open house is the day after Thanksgiving, by the way, and you're all invited." She opened her arms wide in a way that included all of us. "And then, here you come along and ask me to help you out, Jack. I didn't see how I was going to get everything done, so I'm so, so lucky I ran into Mitch Bloom the other day and told him I was looking for someone to help, and there—tah-dah!"

Zio's white face and black head popped out from behind a frame.

"*Zio!*" All of us from the Gallery School were amazed.

"Can't get away from me, can ya?" he asked with a grin.

Even though he was twice as big as Merla, he looked like an embarrassed little kid.

"Said he could work evenings and some weekends, and what is soooo fabulous is he already knows a lot about hanging paintings because of his work at the gallery," said Merla. "And," she went on, "he has such a good eye. He's given me some great feedback on my own work."

"I like art," he mumbled shyly.

Merla clapped her hands and got businesslike. "But, okay, we have a lot to accomplish. This is our one and only shot at this, but first, maybe I should find out who you all are."

Jack told us to introduce ourselves, although Merla had already met Liesl because of Liesl working on the mural. In her overalls and blonde hair Merla actually looked a lot like I thought Liesl might look one day.

"Now," Merla said, "Zio has prepared all these flats, and it's up to you to paint a jungle on them. Here are some paintings by the famous French painter Henri Rousseau," she said, opening an art book and holding it up. "This is the mood of what you're looking for, right, Jack?" He nodded, and she went on. "Large, pointy-leaved plants. Bright colored flowers. Exotic fruit. Sketch first." She gave us each some chalk. "Can't make a mistake with chalk. Use big arm movements. Let it flow. No fussy, fuddy-duddy, little-old-lady details. Think *big*. Liesl, you show us."

Liesl grinned happily. Taking her piece of chalk, she reached toward the blank canvas and, moving her whole skinny body, created an entire tropical-looking bush in about two seconds.

"That's supposed to make us feel confident?" Wildman asked.

Pretty soon all of us were spread out all over the room working on sections. It was actually fun once you got past the first scary mark. I liked the feeling of the chalk on the canvas, kind of smooth and crushy at the same time.

Jack and Aunt Bridget and Zio stood by, making suggestions. Merla occasionally swooped in on someone and yelled, "No, no. No fussy details. No one's going to see that from the audience. Keep it big, keep it big."

Once the whole jungle was outlined, Merla gave us old shirts to put on to protect our clothes and then set us up with paintbrushes and paint. "Don't go wasting that paint." She glared at us. "Only pour out what you need. This is a volunteer job, out of the kindness of my heart because I believe in Jack Mack, but I'll tear you limb from limb if you waste a single drop."

Then everyone was quiet for a while, concentrating, when from over on the other side of the room, I heard, "So the fire lords were coming in the power door, and yo, I forgot to open the treasure chest."

Wildman's voice went on and on. To tell the truth, I was glad I wasn't standing next to him. Most of the time I really couldn't handle his Black Avenger stuff.

At some point Zio disappeared. When he came back, the whole room filled up with the smell of pizza. Everyone instantly stopped working. We sat on the floor eating in front of the scenery, although Dillon, like always, was sitting a little apart from everyone else.

"It looks good, folks," Jack said, stretched out on the floor next to Aunt Bridget. "Performance is creeping up, so just a reminder: I want everybody off book by next rehearsal."

Everyone groaned. We had only heard him say this about a hundred times.

After the pizza we worked for another hour or so before Merla said it was time to stop and clean up.

"Hey, Gareth, want to go over to the rink after this?" I asked. He and Liesl and I were standing side by side over a big sink washing brushes in a room where Merla taught a painting class. "They're making the ice. I'm going to stop by on my way home."

"Oh, wow, that's right, the Zamboni's coming tonight." Gareth looked excited for a moment, but then he seemed to think of something. "I don't know . . ." He took off his cap and rubbed his head and put the cap back on.

Gabriela came in just then. "Okay, Gary, I'm ready," she said. She walked over and looped her arm through Gareth's.

"*Gary?* What the *heck*?" Liesl's eyes sparked.

"Later, buddy," Gareth said to me, shrugging slightly with an embarrassed smile.

"Whoa," said Liesl as we stood and watched them go off together. "Come on," she said with a smirk. "Let's go to the rink."

Liesl and I told Aunt Bridget where we were going, then we ran down the Art Factory stairs and zipped over to the park.

It was a clear, cold night, good, I hoped, for making ice, even though Mitch had said good ice didn't depend on cold so much as the time of year and position of the sun—the lower in the sky the better.

It was a bit of a hike to the rink, but it was fun to be out. It seemed like everyone in Gloria was in the park and headed for the same place we were, some with little kids, some with dogs. Just up ahead we even saw Old Violet trundling along, pushing her cart.

I realized with a rush of relief that the Blue Gang was done—no more spray-painting.

I stopped by a tree and patted it.

"What are you doing?" Liesl asked.

"I'm just saying hello to the park," I said. "Telling it I like it."

"You're a weirdo," she said.

twenty-four

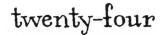

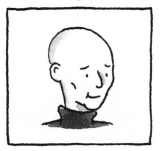

If kids can learn to be other people,

they can learn to be themselves.

—Jack Mack

What Jack Mack meant by "off book" was that he wanted us to know the lines, not carry the script with us onstage anymore.

The next few rehearsals were terrible. Gareth, especially, was struggling big-time. In the play the String Man is supposed to play cat's cradle with string, so both his hands have to be free. Gareth didn't want to let go of the script. Jack, getting a little hot under the collar, ordered Gareth to put down the script and just do the string games without saying the lines.

Gareth started off okay, his fingers flicking back and forth as he looped the string on them, setting up the first round of the game. He held his hands up for Gabriela, who dived right in.

On his turn Gareth sort of lunged into the string. His fingers looped wildly, and then when he held up his hands, he had a sheepish grin on his face. Gabriela took one look at the mess and said, "Holy tamale, scrambled eggs!"

Everyone else laughed, but Jack's shoulders hunched, and he wasn't smiling at all. "Gareth, you haven't learned the string games," he said.

"Don't worry, I'm going to learn them," said Gareth.

"And you haven't learned your lines." Jack got up from his chair and started pacing.

"Yeah, I know, I know."

Jack blew out a big breath.

The rest of us were quiet. I felt torn between feeling embarrassed for Gareth and amazed. I never expected him to be the one having so much trouble.

Aunt Bridget was the one who suggested Gareth come over on Saturday morning and work with Jack when no one else was around except Aunt Bridget and me.

I sat at Aunt Bridget's worktable, staring at my essay, hoping to finish it before they arrived. I looked at all the big question marks and comments JinYoung Kim had put in all over the place. I put my head down on the table.

Aunt Bridget was at her sewing machine working on Liesl's monkey costume. She had found fuzzy material that didn't shed the way the gorillas had, and she was happy about that.

"Uh-oh, what's the matter?" she asked.

I lifted my head and sighed. "I'm writing this paper over for the fourth time," I said. "Everything I write isn't good enough."

Aunt Bridget smiled sympathetically. "Oh, I know how that goes." She went back to her sewing.

I had seen Aunt Bridget start stuff over that she'd sewn wrong. She usually stomped around for a bit. Sometimes she threw things, but then she got back down to it.

"Mr. Kim always says I should revise stuff five hundred times."

"Listen," Aunt Bridget said, looking at her watch, "Jack and Gareth are coming over to rehearse in exactly fifty-two minutes. See if you can fit at least eighty-two of your five hundred revisions in before they come."

"Yes, ma'am." I gripped my pen and looked at the paper.

I dived in this time, into all the ideas that were swirling like water inside my head. I let them wash all over me for a minute, and then I started swimming.

If I wrote a good sentence that perfectly said what I was trying to say, then it was like I was doing the crawl. If it was so-so, then I was doing the breaststroke. If it was bad but at least better than nothing, then it was the doggy paddle. Sometimes I had to tread water just to keep my head up.

But all of a sudden I began to feel like I had something to say. I wasn't just putting words down on paper to complete the assignment.

By the time I heard footsteps on the stairs, I didn't want to stop. As Jack came into the apartment Aunt Bridget pointed at me and then put her finger up to her lips and said, "Shhh." When Gareth came plowing into the room, Aunt Bridget went through the same thing with him.

I didn't lift my head from the paper. I had to keep swimming until I reached the other side.

I don't know how much time went by, but I know that when I finally wrote the last sentence, my fingers hurt from gripping the pen. I put it down and looked up at everyone.

"All done?" Aunt Bridget asked brightly.

"For now," I said. I knew there were a few things I wanted to fix up. I also knew I didn't care anymore if Mr. Kim liked what I had written. I liked it.

"All right, then, Gareth," said Jack, standing up. He pushed up the sleeves of the turtleneck he was wearing.

"I'm not good at acting," said Gareth. He sat at the table and sank his head into his hands. He looked just the way I think I must have looked an hour earlier.

"Look," said Jack, "I wouldn't have cast you as the String Man if I didn't believe you could do it."

"I'm not anything like the String Man," said

Gareth. "I'm not funny. Willy is funny. He should play the String Man."

It was hard for me to believe Gareth thought I was better at something than he was.

Jack pushed back his chair and stood up. "Come on, old boy, the truth is you're still groping for the lines. How can you have fun with the part if you're trying to remember the lines?"

Gareth groaned slightly. "You just said I should be working harder."

"Yes, work hard, and then you can play with it. A play is a *play*."

Gareth looked miserable. "I'm sorry," he said. "I know how you feel. Sometimes I pick certain kids to pitch, and I get really surprised when they buckle under pressure."

"So what do you do?" Jack asked.

"I tell 'em to pretend they're someone else, someone who couldn't possibly get nervous, like, say, Waldo Yadzinski."

Jack thumped Gareth on his back. "Hey, coach! Good idea!" He pulled a chair out from Aunt Bridget's worktable and set it in the middle of the living room. "Go sit in that chair, Gareth."

"Okay," he said, not very enthusiastically. He went and sat in the chair.

"All right. Now, Willy, you be yourself, and Gareth, you be Old Violet."

"*Old Violet?*"

"Go on, Willy."

I started walking across the room. Gareth grabbed

a piece of Aunt Bridget's fabric and put it on his head like one of Old Violet's scarves. He sat hunched over, his eyes sort of rolling in his head. "Is that you, Willy Wilson?" He spoke in a hoarse voice. "You're a big boy now, HA! Do something about the park, do you hear me? DO YOU HEAR ME?" He pointed to his teeth. "You see my teeth? My boyfriend made them for me."

"Oh, good grief!" I practically fell over.

"What is the matter with you?"

"TEETH!" I yelled. "Old Violet!"

I got up and grabbed Gareth by the arms and started leaping around the room.

"He's gone mad," said Aunt Bridget. "And I'm the one who's going to have to tell his parents."

"*He helps the homeless not to frown.* That's the clue!" I shouted. "I bet if I can find out who gave Old Violet her dentures—"

"Hey, that's great!" said Aunt Bridget, who had been trying to figure out with me who the dentist could possibly be. We'd even begun phoning dentists starting with the letter *A,* asking if Otto Pettingill had been their patient.

I wanted to race out of the house and find Dillon immediately, but I knew I had to hang on for a while longer. Both Jack and Gareth had this I'm-just-waiting-for-you-to-be-finished look on their faces.

"So," said Jack, "take your script, Gareth, and find the part where the String Man first comes in, and deliver the lines like Old Violet would."

Gareth shook his head in disbelief.

"Go on, do it."

"HA! Be quiet, I have exciting news for you!" Gareth used the Old Violet voice and got up and began thumping around the room.

"All right, keep going, but be Belle Vera this time."

Gareth plumped his hands on his waist, and with an exaggerated thick French accent he said, "Give me some string and I will tell you. You won't be sorry. It's very, very important news. A secret."

"Good," said Jack. "Now say your next bunch of lines like Liesl would. Pani has just given you the string."

Gareth took a breath, and then he launched into the lines. "You must listen very, very, very, very, very carefully. Eight years ago, in your village, twins were born. But it is very, very, very, very, very bad luck to have twins born to a village." Gareth did Liesl being really nice and then suddenly losing her temper and then being really nice again. My stomach began to ache from laughing. Aunt Bridget had tears running down her face.

"All right, next batch of lines and be Mitch Bloom."

Gareth drew himself up, so he seemed taller. He raised a long, skinny arm in the air. He made his voice deep. "Shhh, we must be very, very, very quiet because the birds will hear. They have, you know, been corrupted by the field mice, and they do not know how to keep a secret."

"One last thing. Be yourself coaching the team and do the speech you give when you're leaving."

This time Gareth was intense and focused. "Believe

what you like, my dear, but if you wish, I can tell you more. But, oh my, that leaf, that slug, they are telling me it's time to go."

"Okay, now say all those lines again while you flash your teeth like Old Violet; stretch out your words like Belle Vera, with just a hint of the accent; lose your temper like Liesl; feel long and skinny like Mitch; and be just as bossy as Gareth Pugh when he's coaching his team."

Gareth went through the lines one more time. He knew them now and didn't need the script. There was a crazy light in his eyes, and the freckles on his face were bouncing.

We clapped when he finished.

"You found him," said Jack, a big smile on his face. "You found the String Man inside of you."

Gareth looked happy, too. "To tell the truth, that was the most fun I've had since we started working on this play."

"Ah," said Jack. He rubbed the top of his shiny head, looking pleased.

"What's different?" asked Aunt Bridget.

Gareth scratched an ear, looking thoughtful. "I guess not everyone else is here." He blushed, his freckles almost disappearing under the redness.

"Ahhhh, so that's it," said Jack again, nodding in a knowing sort of way. "It's tough when you fall for a dame. You're no longer your own person." He glanced at Aunt Bridget. Aunt Bridget ducked her head toward the mask she was working on. "But I do believe that if you really know what you're doing, like under your skin, like in your bones, then a certain girl's presence will torment you less."

Gareth slouched forward, but then he sat back and said defiantly, "But it's also Dillon Deronda. I hate working with him. No one likes him, and that's a fact."

"Hans Zerbe likes him," I said. "When we went there looking for the clue, Hans Zerbe gave him Waldo Yadzinski's glove."

"What?" I thought Gareth was going to explode. "Why would he do that? Give it to Dillon, I mean?"

"He kept saying how Dillon has passion."

"I have passion, too." Gareth started pacing frantically around the room.

"Yeah, for Gabriela," I couldn't help saying.

Gareth lunged, and a pile of fabric went flying.

"Will you get out of here?" Aunt Bridget said, exasperated.

"Let's go look for the next clue," I said.

"Really?" asked Gareth. "You mean, you're actually going to let me go with you instead of that ratfaced creep who thinks he's the best thing since the Yad?"

"Not instead of," I said, *"with.* Dillon has to come, too. It's his painting. Come on, we have to go find him."

twenty-five

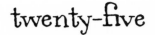

Sometimes I dream I'm inside a giant mouth
and I'm hiking over a range of molars.

—*Dennis Quick*

"OLD VIOLET!" I yelled as Gareth and I raced
toward her on our bikes.

She was sitting on her bench, the shopping cart
parked beside her. "Don't you go calling me old," she
screeched at me.

"Your teeth," I said. "Where'd you get your teeth?"

Old Violet instantly stopped being a grouchy old
lady. She batted her eyes and smiled a big, fake smile.
"Bee-yoo-ti-full teeth, ain't they?" she said, flashing
them at us. "My boyfriend gave them to me."

Gareth and I looked at each other. "What's your
boyfriend's name?" I asked.

"Dennis," Old Violet said, patting her kerchief, smiling away.

"Does he have a last name?" I held my breath. Would she even know his last name?

"Does he have a last name?" Old Violet started cackling. "Of course he has a last name. Don't you have a last name?" A couple of pigeons waddled toward us, looking for treats.

"Yes, but what is it?"

"Don't you know your own last name?"

"Yes, I know my own last name," I said, breathing hard, trying not to lose it. Gareth, hanging on to his bike, was laughing his head off. "What's your boyfriend's last name? Dennis what?"

"Dennis the Dentist," said Old Violet, cackling again.

"Come on, let's go," Gareth said, pulling me by the arm. "What a stupid conversation."

We started to ride away. "QUICK!" Old Violet screeched.

Gareth and I automatically jerked our bikes to one side, thinking someone was about to run us over.

"It's QUICK!" she screeched again, waving her arms wildly. "My boyfriend's name is Dennis Quick."

I grabbed Gareth's arm. "Dennis Quick," I said.

"Let's call and find out if he's there," said Gareth. "I've got my cell."

We leaned our bikes against a bench, and Gareth dug into his pocket for his phone. He called Information and then punched in the numbers. He nodded to show me that someone on the other end had answered. "Is Dr. Quick in his office today?" He nodded at me again, giving a thumbs-up. "Well, do you think it's okay if a few kids come in and ask him a few questions about dentists for a school paper?" He nodded again. "Great, thanks. Oh, and what's the address? Great, we'll be over." Gareth grinned at me. "That was clever about the school paper, don't you think?" His confidence level was definitely back up a few notches. "His office is over in the East Park. Must be pretty near to where Mr. Pettingill used to live."

"Come on, we have to find Dillon." I climbed back on my bike and took off.

"HEY!" Gareth yelled. "Wait up."

We found Dillon working on the roof of the rink house with Mitch and a bunch of other people.

"Hey, Willy, we're almost done," Mitch called down happily. "Thought we might celebrate Thanksgiving here in the rink house."

I liked that idea a whole lot but wondered if Mom would go for it. We usually went to Granny and Grandpa's house.

"Got news for you," I called up to Dillon.

He scrambled down from the roof, and I told him we thought we had found the dentist.

"Score," he said, jerking up a thumb.

Telling Mitch he'd be gone for a few hours, Dillon went to get his bike, which was leaning against the new rink house.

"He's coming?" he asked, eyeing Gareth suspiciously.

"Hey," Gareth said, scowling. "I'm the one who found out where he works."

Dillon only grunted. "Got yourself a Cadillac," he said, nodding at Gareth's bike, which was brand-new. "Not too shabby." Dillon's looked old and beat-up and too small for him. "Life must be tough."

Gareth shrugged and didn't say anything. We got on our bikes and started riding. We saw Liesl on the way, bent over the sidewalk, drawing with chalk. A group of little kids surrounded her, watching.

"Keep going," said Dillon. "We don't want her along."

"Yeah, we do," said Gareth. He stopped, just to bug Dillon, of course. We wheeled our bikes over to where she was crouched, while Dillon, muttering under his breath, made a point of keeping his distance.

Liesl was drawing a little kid who was sitting on a bench facing her. She had captured him perfectly—how his hair stuck up and the way his ears stuck out and the little crooked smile on his face.

"We're working on the treasure hunt," said Gareth. "Want to come along?"

Liesl took a penny out of the apron pocket where she kept her chalk. Tossing it up in the air, she said, "Tails I come, heads I don't." She caught the coin and slapped it over onto the back of her hand. "It's heads, but I'll come anyway. Just give me two shakes of a rat's tail while I put this stuff away. Hey kids, I'm done for the day. Come back tomorrow."

The kids began to whine and complain, especially the boy she had been drawing. "SCAT!" she yelled, stamping her foot and shaking her fists at them.

"We're on bikes," said Gareth.

179

"I've got a bike," she said. "Right here." It was leaning up against the toolshed. "I just saw Zio," she added. "He was coming out of there." She nodded in the direction of the shed. "I guess he's helping Mitch with the rink."

We hopped on our bikes and headed across the park. For the middle of November, it was pretty nice out. I was wearing an old wool cap of Uncle Roger's, but I was beginning to feel like I didn't need it anymore.

Dennis Quick's office building wasn't that far from Wanda's Wigs and Specs. Gareth attached his new bike to a lamppost, fiddling for what seemed like forever with a new high-tech lock. The rest of us didn't think anyone would take our bikes. We just left them leaning against the building.

"We're not allowed to ask about the clue, so we're here researching the lives of dentists," I told Dillon and Liesl as we went in the main door.

We walked down a hallway and found a glass door that said Dr. Dennis Quick, D.M.D., in black letters. There was also a handwritten note taped to the door that said, "I work Monday through Friday from ten to eight and most of the time on Saturday mornings unless I decide to pack up and ride my Harley out to the country and go fishing."

We stepped into a waiting area, and a woman sitting behind the front desk looked up. "Yes can I— Oh, are you the kids? Dr. Quick is just letting the Novocain set in. Dr. Quick," she called out. "Those kids are here."

Dr. Quick came strolling out of a room and down a narrow hallway to the front desk and the waiting area. He was tall, with thick black hair and a long sharp nose. He was wearing latex gloves.

"Howdy-doo, kids, what can I do for you today?" He greeted us with a big grin, showing us a mouthful of the most crooked teeth I had ever seen. They were all crowded in, overlapping each other. I tried not to stare, but it was hard.

Gareth pulled his script from his back pocket and pretended to refer to it. "We're writing a report about the lives of dentists, and we just wanted to ask you a few questions."

"Fire away," said Dr. Quick. "I have a small window of opportunity here. Got a fellow in there who couldn't sleep on account of a bad toothache, and I'm trying to help him out. Just letting the numbness set in so I can get to work."

"Well," said Gareth, "the first question is, what do you like best about being a dentist?"

Dr. Quick gave a great big, crooked grin. "That's easy. Helping people chew," he said.

"The second question is . . . um . . . what unusual cases have you handled?"

"Unusual cases," said Dr. Quick, snapping the ends of the latex fingers as he thought. He looked at his assistant. "Well, Sheila, I know we've had our fair share—"

"There was that boy who broke his front tooth on the seesaw," Sheila said.

"Oh yes," said Dr. Quick. "That's right. His parents

weren't home, so his older brother tried to glue the broken bit on with superglue."

"It ended up getting stuck to his finger," said Sheila.

Dr. Quick nodded. "And then there was the fellow who wanted me to replace his own set with wooden teeth he'd carved himself. He figured he'd never get cavities that way, and he could just sand them now and then to get them looking nice again."

"I think he had a thing for George Washington," said Sheila.

A dentist's life was more interesting than I had realized. I almost forgot to be looking for the clue. But there was Dillon slinking around while Dr. Quick was talking. He disappeared down the hallway. Liesl melted away, following him.

I was beginning to be a little worried because, after all, we didn't know for sure this was the right dentist, when Dr. Quick said, "And then there was Old Violet in the park. Otto Pettingill asked me if I could do something about her teeth. *That* was an experience. I've been her true love ever since and—"

We heard a noise from the room where Dillon and Liesl had gone.

Both Dillon and Liesl came down the hall with wild expressions on their faces. "Roland Brookings is in there," Liesl said tensely, the blue vein lit up over her nose, her face red. "I never wanted to see that slimy creep again in my life. Come on, I'm not staying here."

twenty-six

Sometimes my whole life feels like a toothache.
 —*Roland N. Brookings, Jr.*

Mr. Brookings was in the hallway now, dentist bib flying up around his neck, his red hair standing on end. "Wha ah you doooin' heah?" The Novocain had numbed up his mouth, and he had rubbery lips. He took us all in, Gareth, Liesl, Dillon, me. I shrank back, looking around wildly, and there, high up on a bookcase behind Sheila, I saw a jaw, one of those models dentists have, a little piece of folded up paper clenched between its teeth.

I nudged Gareth. "The clue," I whispered.

"Where?" he asked, looking around.

"Di you fawow me heah?" Mr. Brookings was trying to yell past his numbness.

Dr. Quick took a step toward him. "Now, Mr. Brookings, calm down," he said soothingly. "Go sit down. I'm sure the Novocain is ready now." Dr. Quick pushed him back down the hallway. "Sheila, come give me a hand, won't you?"

Muffled shouts continued to come from the room.

"The clue is *there,* in the jaw," I said, pointing. Gareth darted behind the desk before I could. Reaching up, he pulled the piece of paper out, and the whole jaw came crashing down.

"Oops," I said picking up the pieces. "All the teeth fell out."

"What are you kids doing?" Sheila came rushing back down the hallway.

I hurriedly stuck the teeth back into the jaw. "Just wanted to look. SORRY!" I yelled.

We ran out of the office and down the stairs. Outside, Dillon, Liesl, and I grabbed our bikes, not waiting for Gareth, who was struggling with his lock. Once back in the park we stopped and breathed a bit, waiting for him.

"What was that slimy creep doing there?" Liesl asked.

"He had a toothache!" I said.

"He's the guy," Dillon was saying.

"What guy?" asked Gareth, who finally came riding up.

"After my father . . ." Dillon swallowed hard and then started again. "After my family's painting disappeared, I went around to antique stores looking for it. And that guy was at one of them. I remember because of his red hair. And because he was, like, into listening to all my questions, even though he was pretending not to."

"Did you describe the painting in front of him?" I asked. "Like details?"

"Yeah, man, that's it." Dillon nodded. "Yeah, I get it now."

"I get it now, too," I said.

"What do you get?" Gareth asked, looking annoyed.

"That guy is Roland Brookings, Jr.," I said to Dillon, ignoring Gareth for the moment. "He used to be Otto Pettingill's lawyer."

"The one who tried to buy the park with Frank Featherstone," said Dillon.

"Right," I said.

Dillon clenched his fists. "I ought to go right back up there and knock out all his teeth."

"Yeah," said Liesl. "I'll help you."

"I'm going to knock out all *your* teeth unless you tell me what's going on." Gareth got off his bike and looked at me threateningly.

A bunch of older guys tossing a football and yelling to each other jogged toward us. I waited until they went past, and then I explained how we had always wondered how Frank Featherstone knew what the painting looked like. Now it seemed pretty clear that Brookings had overheard Dillon talking about it, and that he and Featherstone had decided to pretend they had it.

"Okay, so now what?" asked Gareth.

"Well, now we know for sure those guys don't

have the painting," I said. "So Mr. Pettingill did buy it, and we're on the right track with the treasure hunt. Gareth, you do have the clue, don't you?" I panicked suddenly, worried that in the rush to get out of there, we had left it behind.

The clue was in Gareth's hand. He unfolded it and read,

"With a paintbrush in her hand,
She's a magician of the land.
Sally Simpkins was her name
Before she garnered fame.
The treasure's there
Within her care."

"Sally Simpkins! That's Merla!" I said. We all looked at each other. "Wow, I can't believe it. The painting's been with her the whole time."

"Hey, where's rat-face going?" Liesl pointed to Dillon, who was on his bike and speeding away.

"Let's go," said Gareth.

We scrambled for our bikes and took off after Dillon to the art factory. I felt the cold air rushing against my face, and I couldn't help being excited. I thought of Lena and Leo, the expressions on their faces when they got their *tesoro* back!

Leaving our bikes in the lobby, we sprinted up the stairs. Dillon was standing in the hallway facing Zio, who was hulking in Merla's doorway. Neither of them looked very happy.

"She's not here," Dillon said, clenching his fists. "And he won't let me in."

"When will she be back?" I asked.

"Not until next week," Zio said slowly and heavily. He glared at Dillon. "I told him."

"But where is she?" I asked.

"Taking a break," said Zio. "Getting rested up for the exhibition. I'm hanging her paintings for her." He rocked on his feet, still filling up the doorway.

"Listen, Zio, I left some things here," said Liesl. She stepped in front of Dillon and tugged on Zio's arm. "Okay if I come in and get them?"

"For you, no problem." Zio stepped out of the way.

Liesl marched into the loft, and we followed. Zio put up a hand and blocked Dillon's way. "Not you, buddy."

"What?" Dillon's face and neck turned a blotchy red. "You can't stop me."

"Ya wanna bet?" Zio crossed his big arms and spread his feet apart. "Let's see just how tough you are, big guy."

"Just wait there, Dillon," I said. "We'll look around."

We stepped into the loft.

Gareth turned to me. "What's his beef with Dillon, anyway?"

"I'm not sure," I said. I remembered how Zio had told Dillon to wise up the last time he had seen him. "Maybe he knows somehow that Dillon was part of the Blue Gang."

We were standing in the large, open space where we had worked on the scenery.

"Let's just spread out and look everywhere," said Gareth.

There were a couple of rooms, one full of easels and painting materials, another full of clay heads and sculpting tools. We went through the shelves and even opened closets. There was no sign of a small painting of Saint Francis.

The last room we couldn't even get into. Gareth wrestled with the doorknob until I thought he was going to break it. We went back to the doorway where Zio was still standing and asked him about the locked room.

"That's Merla's own studio," said Zio. "You're not going to get in there."

"I might have left my stuff in there," said Liesl. "You must have keys, Zio. Can't you please open it for us?" She looked at him with her blue eyes wide open. She could look very innocent when she wanted to.

"No way. Just have to wait. Like I said, she'll be back next week for her open house. Now you all get going so I can get back to work."

We walked down the stairs and stood in the lobby of the Art Factory. The jaw muscles on Dillon's face were working away. Then he jammed his hands into his pockets. "My father's in the hospital," he said. "He had a cold, and then it turned into bronchitis and then pneumonia and then, I don't know, something even worse. My grandmother says he keeps talking about the painting, like he's feeling guilty." He hunched his shoulders. "Don't know if he'll make it to next week."

twenty-seven

Someone told me that some guy wanted to buy
the park so he could build more buildings.
Is this guy crazy, or what?
—*Old Violet*

We sat around the long tables we had helped Mitch
set up in the rink house. Liesl and I had helped
Mitch and Belle and Zio set them with plates and
glasses and silverware loaned to us by Gareth's
family.

It was cold outside, but a fire was blazing in the
fireplace inside. So many people were crammed in
together, and with so much hot food on the table,

and candles, too, giving off heat, it wasn't long before the windows steamed up and people were taking off their jackets and sweaters.

I looked around. It was an amazing collection of people: Mom and Dad, Granny and Grandpa, Aunt Bridget, Jack and Zack Mack, Liesl and Gareth and Gareth's sister and his parents, Hans Zerbe and Clara, Franz, and Wolfgang, who roamed around under the table, bumping up against people's legs until Mr. Zerbe ordered them to lie down. Gabriela and Fernando were there, and their mother, and Itsuko. Itsuko had purple eyes today.

Oh, and Ernesto Peligroso. Fernando made sure we set a place for him.

Mitch, Belle, and Zio came bursting in, holding platters high. "*Monsieurs et dames*, ladies and gentlemen," Belle called out, her cheeks rosy and her eyes sparkling, "we present to you two whole turkeys and three ducks—roasted in our very own Gill Park oven!"

Everyone clapped as they set the platters down.

Mitch stood at the head of the table and asked everyone to join hands. Then he said quietly, "We have Otto Pettingill to thank for our being here today, on this island of earth in the middle of the city of Gloria. You provide the right growing environment, and all kinds of plants can coexist—the plain and the exotic, the humble and the lofty. There are young plants and old. . . ." His Adam's apple bobbed, and he couldn't finish.

"And as one of the old shrubs, I say *merci*, thank you, and amen," Belle said, finishing for him.

I felt my hands being squeezed by Gareth and Liesl, who were sitting on either side of me.

Spread out all over the table were bowls and dishes and platters full of all the food people had brought—Mom's cranberry sauce; Granny and Grandpa's home-made pickles; Gabriela's mom's rice dish with peas and tiny shrimps and mussels; Gareth's dad's baked yams with baby marshmallows, famous, Gareth said, throughout the city of Gloria. Hans Zerbe had brought a couple of jars of marinated chestnuts. He said he had carried them over from Germany in 1975. It was funny thinking that I would be eating something that was older than I was. Aunt Bridget had whipped up a Mount Everest of mashed potatoes. Belle had brought dandelion wine, which she said Zio had helped her make, and Mitch had brought green beans and peas which he had picked from his own garden and then frozen. Itsuko brought sushi, which caused a big argument between Gareth's dad and my dad—my dad saying it wasn't safe to eat sushi and Mr. Pugh saying that was nonsense: If you ate sushi, you could live to be one hundred.

Itsuko said, "That's true. I'm ninety-nine, you know." She gleamed her purple eyes at Dad.

Belle had baked a couple of loaves of bread, and there were special rice cakes Mr. Kim's family had prepared for us.

For dessert we had apple and blueberry and

mincemeat pies, all made by Mitch and baked in the Gill Park oven.

It was the best Thanksgiving feast I'd ever had, and I stuffed myself.

After dinner Hans Zerbe stood up and said he was going to offer his thanks for a wonderful meal by playing some music. He had brought a violin with him, but to my surprise, he played it like a fiddle and got us all clapping and tapping our feet. When he was finished, he turned to me and said, "All right, maestro, it's your turn now."

I didn't want to play at all, but then Gareth and Liesl and Gabriela started banging on the table. "Play, Willy, play! Play, Willy, play! We won't shut up until you get up!"

"Please, Willy, play something so they'll be quiet," said Dad.

I took the violin from Hans. I was relieved to see it wasn't the Stradivarius. I decided I'd play what I knew best—my own tune again. I played it twice through, warming up to it. I liked playing my park song right in the middle of my own park.

At the end everyone clapped loudly, the kids banging on the table again. I realized that Mr. Kim must have come in while I was playing. He was sitting next to my mother, clapping, too, with a big smile on his face.

Then we cleared everything away to the little kitchen in the back of the rink house and washed dishes. It was actually fun, a couple of us standing over the sink with soapy water up to our elbows while everyone else dried or just stood around and joked and talked, or argued, like Mr. Pugh and Dad were arguing now about whether or not it was better to cut your toenails straight across or curve them.

When every last plate, glass, fork, knife, and spoon had been washed, Mitch said, "Come on, the rink's open for skating." Some people, like Gareth, had their own stuff, but most of us used gear Mitch had been collecting all fall.

"Come on, Marcia, get yourself out there," said Dad. "You used to be a wonderful skater."

"I haven't skated in years," Mom said, but then she went over to Mitch's stash and found a pair of skates that fit her.

There had been an announcement in the paper about the opening of the rink on Thanksgiving, and soon a crowd collected. A bunch of the Gorillas came, and a whole bunch of kids I recognized as Sharks.

It was growing dark by this time, but the rink was brightly lit with floodlights. Mitch had also strung little lights from post to post, so there was an exciting, Christmasy feeling about everything. Music was coming from Mr. P.'s apartment, two violins and a cello, a deep warm sound matching the smell of roasted meat and pies, which still hung in the air.

Mom skated around in a baby blue fleece jacket and hat. Her cheeks were rosy, and she looked as excited as a little kid. "Watch this, Willy!" I couldn't believe it. She did this graceful, ballet-looking thing on one foot. She laughed at the expression on my face.

Jack Mack and Aunt Bridget were ice dancing, side by side, hand in hand, feet and legs coordinated like they had been a pairs couple all their lives. Fernando was learning to skate, pushing a chair around. Mr. Zerbe and Belle sat by the bread oven with the dogs at their feet.

Marnie and Kizzi showed up together. Marnie started teaching Kizzi, Gabriela, and Liesl to skate. They were all leaning on each other and laughing their heads off.

I had only skated at home at an indoor rink. It was so much better outside, with the sun going down, the sky overhead turning pink, the cool air against my face.

Seeing Mitch leaning against a post, arms folded, taking it all in, I skated over to him.

"It's really great, Mitch!" I said.

"It's the best!" Mitch agreed. "Everything I hoped it would be." His nose was red from the cold, giving him a happy glow. "Hey, look at that!"

We watched as Liesl, in a bright red hat, her ankles turning in, her whole little skinny body straining to stay up, made it almost over to us without falling, then pitched forward into Mitch.

"Bravo," said Mitch, catching her. "You'll be ready for the Olympics before the night is over."

Liesl's cheeks were as red as her hat, and her blue eyes were blazing with excitement. Then she made a face and said, "You know how you said all kinds of plants can grow here?" Mitch nodded. "Well, I guess ratty weeds can grow here, too," she said, pointing to Dillon, who had just appeared.

Just behind Dillon were Leo and Lena and half a dozen other people who were Derondas, I guessed. They were all walking arm in arm, chattering happily, pointing to the oven, explaining their work on the bricks.

"Oh, you never know with weeds," said Mitch. "Sometimes they end up turning into flowers you sort of like."

"Talk about weeds, isn't that Frank Featherstone?" I asked.

"Yikes," said Mitch, turning to look.

Frank Featherstone was standing a few yards away from the rink, over on the other side, watching everything. He was wearing a long winter overcoat, the collar turned up. His big, flabby face was almost too big for the rest of his body. But then Gareth shot by, landing a hefty punch on my right shoulder, and I took off after him. Next time I thought of looking for Frank Featherstone, he was gone.

Dillon was now sitting on a bench putting skates on. Gareth called out to him. "Hey, hotshot, how about a game? Gorillas against the Sharks?"

One end of the rink was roped off for hockey. In a few minutes Gareth had organized us. He was back to being confident and bossy, assigning kids we didn't know to teams, laying down a bunch of rules.

We started up, zooming around, sticks from Mitch's stash clacking against each other. Zack kept switching sides randomly. "Can't decide which team I'm on," he said, his face lit up with a crazy grin.

Even in hockey Gareth and Dillon were the best players. I guess it didn't matter what sport they played. They were both coordinated and totally competitive. The score was six to seven, Sharks ahead, when Zack accidentally whaled into Dillon and sent him flying. We all stopped skating and waited, holding our breath to see how Dillon was going to take it. He sort of flailed around for a minute, and then we realized he was laughing. He was laughing so hard he couldn't get back up on his feet. We all looked at each other. I don't think any of us had ever heard Dillon laugh like that.

As the action started up again, I leaned against the boards for a minute and just watched. I wished I had Liesl's talent at drawing. I wanted to freeze this moment, the ice rink full of little kids and big kids, grown-ups and old people. The skaters skated, the watchers watched and talked, curls of smoke rose up out of the chimneys of the rink house and the bake oven. Old Violet sat on a bench with a plate heaped high with food that Zio had given her. A sliver of moon hung overhead. The music flowed out of Mr. P.'s apartment.

I didn't know if Mr. P.'s spirit was in the moon or the music, but wherever he was, I bet he liked what was happening in his park.

twenty-eight

Sometimes you just have to open your
mouth and see what comes out of it.
—*Liesl Summer*

Merla's open house was at her loft. Dillon and I were both going, counting on finally, finally finding the painting.

Since we were supposed to dress up, I wore the blazer I used to have to wear on Mondays at my old school. Zack and Gareth were both wearing turtlenecks, and Liesl said she was going to be a geek for this occasion. She wore a yellow turtleneck and a long red skirt and sneakers.

Aunt Bridget studied her and then said, "Actually, I think you look pretty cool."

Mom, Dad, Aunt Bridget, Zack, Gareth, and Liesl and I went in Jack's van. As we drove into the parking lot behind the Art Factory we could see it was packed with cars.

A big sign on an easel outside Merla's studio door read WELCOME TO SPART. Merla herself was standing just inside wearing a long, shimmery blue dress with silver stars and crescent moons all over it. Her hair was freshly dyed, almost a whitish blonde, and miniature paintbrushes dangled from her ears. "Oh, darlings, you're here," she exclaimed as we walked in. "Enjoy, enjoy!"

The paintings were hanging in the big space where we had worked on the scenery. It was crammed with people, men in suits and women in slinky dresses. College-age kids in white shirts and black pants were passing around trays loaded with stuff to eat.

Zio was wearing a white shirt and red bow tie. He stood behind a table with a white tablecloth on it, serving drinks.

Gabriela staggered toward us through the crowd. She was wearing heels so high she could barely walk. Wildman was following close behind in a bright yellow jacket. Since I'd never seen him in anything but black before, it almost hurt my eyes to look at him.

"Come on, Gary," Gabriela cooed, just like one of the pigeons in the park. Her hair was up, but a few strands frizzed out around her ears. "Let's go look at the paintings."

Gareth and Gabriela and Wildman disappeared into the crowd.

"Well, that's the end of Gary for the night," said Liesl.

I spotted Kizzi and Marnie standing in a corner, looking at a painting, laughing as always.

"Look at them," said Liesl. "They'll laugh at anything."

I looked around for Dillon, but the place was so jammed with people, it was hard to tell who was or wasn't there. I stared for almost a whole minute at a lady who had bright yellow, curly hair and was wearing the largest pair of glasses I'd ever seen, until it dawned on me that it was Wanda of Wanda's Wigs and Glasses.

"Come on," said Liesl, pulling me by the arm. "We're here to see the paintings, remember?"

The first painting was called *Botticelli Shoots Hoops*.

There were all these basketball players playing in a grove of some kind of fruit trees, a basketball net hung from one of them. There were all these babies with wings, flying around. It looked like a men's team was playing against a women's team. The men were wearing red tunics, which were sort of draped over them, and funny boots with open toes on their feet. The women were in see-through, gauzy white things and barefoot. All the people, the men and the women, looked like beautiful marble statues come to life, and their hair was long and wavy. A man right in the center of the painting was making a shot, the ball sailing out of his hands, heading into the basket. Painted right on the ball was a famous painting I'd seen a lot of a naked woman with long, long, wavy hair standing on a big clamshell that was floating on water.

Itsuko popped up next to us, her eyes matching the silk orange dress she was wearing. "Aren't these marvelous?" she gushed. "Merla has painted each one in the style of the artist. Here is *Monet Playing Croquet in His Garden,*" she said, reading the title of the next painting. "And Merla's painted the garden just the way Monet painted his gardens."

A guy with a beard, a large hat, and a cape was standing in a garden. The flowers were painted with dabs of colors. He was holding a croquet mallet, hitting a ball that had a water lily painted on it.

"Da Vinci's Touchdown," Itsuko said, looking at the next painting. Two teams of football players— one dressed in brown robes, the other in black— were all watching a football soar over the end line of the field. The football had a painting of the *Mona Lisa* on it.

"And this is *Vermeer at the Net,*" said Itsuko, moving along. "He was Dutch, known for the way he captured light." In this one a man in black clothes and a black hat was playing tennis with a woman who had a white cloth covering on her head, so you couldn't see her hair, and she was wearing a blue dress. It looked like if you touched her face, you'd feel the sweat on it. Her eyes gleamed, so she looked like she was really alive. The man was holding his racket up high. The tennis ball was painted with a picture of a girl wearing a pearl earring, her face and eyes and the pearl all catching the light. The ball was sailing high up over the woman's head.

"It's inspired." Cricket Wicklow appeared behind us.

"Wretchedly sly humor," said Trevor.

"Just brilliant," Itsuko agreed.

Liesl grabbed me by the arm and dragged me away. "What are they talking about? Why don't they just admit that Merla is one weird dame. Come on," she said, dragging me along. "There are two more."

The next painting showed a man playing pool, but all the balls were apples. It was called *Cezanne Plays Billards*. It looked more modern than the other paintings because it was made up of all these orange rectangles that made my eyes keep shifting around.

But it was the last one that really caught my attention. It was called *Giotto Hits a Home Run*.

The scene was a baseball game. The players in the outfield were dressed in short blue robes and tights. The batters were wearing red robes and tights. Giotto wasn't holding a bat. He was holding a paintbrush, and he must have just ripped the ball because everyone in the outfield was looking up. The baseball that was flying through the air had a painting on it, too. It was of Saint Francis and the birds.

I felt a tug on my arm, and there was Dillon beside me, looking at the painting. His hair was pulled back, as usual, in a ponytail, but combed. He seemed neater than usual, and older. He was wearing a suit jacket that was too big for him.

"What do we do?" he asked, his face pale.

I looked around. I saw Merla over in a corner. She was surrounded by people, like they were all moths attracted to her brightness. "I don't know," I said.

"Come on," said Liesl. She elbowed her way through the crowd, creating a little path for us over to Merla.

I looked at Dillon. He looked so miserable standing there in his baggy jacket. The sound of all the people talking and laughing seemed too loud. The smell of perfume and drinks and cigarette smoke was getting to me. I wanted to yell, "WHERE'S THE PAINTING?"

Suddenly Liesl did yell. I couldn't believe it. She stood there in her yellow top and long skirt, her mouth wide open, her eyes shut, and screamed her head off. The whole room shut up, everyone stared at her, and then she fell over in a heap on the floor.

"HELP, HELP, HELP!" she screamed.

Dillon and I looked at each other in disbelief.

Merla rushed over to her and bent down. "Stand back, stand back, give her some space," she ordered as everyone tried to cram in and see what was happening.

"Oooh," Liesl said weakly, her eyes fluttering open. "I need water."

"What happened, Liesl?" asked Merla. "Are you all right?"

"Water," she moaned.

"Let's move you out of here," said Merla. "Zio, come and help!"

People moved as Zio swung his big arms through the crowd.

"I'm okay," Liesl said in a panicky way as she saw Zio about to scoop her up. She stood up, holding a hand against her forehead. "I just need to sit down somewhere quiet."

"You come on into my studio," said Merla, holding Liesl by the arm. "I'll be right back," she said to everyone. "Go on, party, have fun. Everything's under control here."

Dillon and I followed as Merla led Liesl out of the room and down a hallway. Jack and Aunt Bridget, Mom and Dad appeared suddenly, too, looking worried.

"Here, come in," said Merla, opening the door that had been locked the day we came looking for the painting. She turned on a light, and we saw a room cluttered with paintings and art materials.

"Here, sit down, Liesl," said Merla. "I'll get you some water."

She whisked some magazines off a couch, and Liesl settled into it, curling her legs underneath her. She caught my eye and started twitching. It took me a moment to realize she was trying to wink.

"What happened to you?" Aunt Bridget asked, coming over to her.

"Something bit me," said Liesl.

"Something bit you?" Jack asked, frowning. "Where?"

"Right in the middle of the floor, where I was standing," said Liesl.

"No, I mean, where did it bite you?"

"On my big toe."

"Let me see," said Jack.

"No, in between my toes," said Liesl, tucking her feet even more beneath her.

"What in the world could have bitten you?" Merla asked as she came over with a glass of water.

"It just hurt so much, I thought I was going to have a *bird*." Liesl stared hard at me. "*Bird,* get it?" Her face was getting red and blotchy.

I finally did get it. Dillon and I looked at each other.

"About the painting—"

"I really liked your paintings, Merla."

Dillon and I started talking at the same moment.

"Oh, that's so nice. Thank you for saying so," said Merla. "I think it's so great when kids are into art. I mean, you have such fresh eyes. Your minds aren't all cluttered with culture, and you—"

"I especially liked the Giotto one, with the baseball that had Saint Francis and the birds on it and all," I said.

"Did you ever see it?" Dillon sort of croaked.

"Did I see what, sweetheart?" Merla asked, taking Liesl's glass. "There, you're looking better. The color's coming back into your face."

"Did you ever see the real painting?" Dillon asked. "The one of Saint Francis and the birds—"

"Did anything in particular inspire you to do the painting of Giotto and Saint Francis and the birds?" I asked.

Merla's little paintbrush earrings swung like crazy as she nodded her head enthusiastically. "Actually, you know, a *darling* little painting of Saint Francis and the birds did come my way. As a matter of fact, it's right . . ." Merla stopped, and her eyebrows squeezed her forehead into worry lines. "That's funny," she said.

"Where is it?" Dillon's hands had formed into fists, and his voice sounded hoarse.

Merla floated across the room. She stood in front of a blank space on the wall. "I don't understand," she said. "It was here. . . . It's been here. . . ." She started looking all around, lifting things off the shelves, poking through paintings. "I can't believe it. This is terrible. Mr. Pettingill asked me to keep it for him . . . until . . . until . . . oh my gosh." Her face was white, her eyebrows pulled down. "He said a boy would come and ask about it." She looked at me and then at Dillon. "Are you . . . is one of you . . ." She rushed around the room, now searching desperately. "Where is it? It was hanging right there for the past two months. A painting doesn't just disappear."

Dillon's face had turned white, and his shoulders were hunched. "It's a setup," he said bitterly. "And you're all a part of it." He looked at me. "You have that painting somewhere. So go ahead and sell it. It's worth big bucks. Go ahead, that's what you wanted all along."

He lunged for the door and disappeared through it. I felt like I'd been kicked.

Merla stood with her hands on her hips. "So what's the story here?"

"It was his painting," I said. My mouth was so dry I could barely speak. "His family's painting. You don't have any idea where it could be?"

Merla shook her head. "I'm so sorry. I don't understand it," she said. "It was there, I swear," she said, pointing to the wall, "from the day Mr. Pettingill brought it to me, to the day I went away. I remember because as I was packing up, I remember looking at it, thinking what a darling little treasure it is."

Treasure. I groaned and sank down on the couch next to Liesl, my head in my hands.

twenty-nine

Stories don't always go the way you want them to. They are like string. Sometimes they get snarled up. Sometimes they get cut.
—*The String Man*

I was lying in bed the next morning, half-dozing, when I heard the phone ring. I could hear Aunt Bridget's voice answering it, and then in a few moments she came into my room. She was wearing Uncle Roger's old bathrobe, and her curly hair was sticking out all over the place.

"That was Mitch," she said. From the expression on her face, I didn't think it was good news. I propped myself up on one elbow. "The Blue Gang attacked the rink and the rink house and the oven last night."

I sat straight up in bed. "Attacked? Like, it's really bad?" I asked, not wanting to know the answer.

Aunt Bridget retied the sash of her bathrobe. "Mitch said it was a disaster. They put salt all over the ice—rock salt." She shook her head, looking really upset. "Mitch said that's about the worst thing you could do to a rink. It's very difficult to get it out."

I felt a little dizzy, and my stomach hurt. "So what did they do to the rink house and the oven?"

"Well, of course, they spray-painted everything blue—the ice, too—after they'd done the damage with the salt. Next they carved stuff into the rink-house logs, and then they took a sledgehammer or something and bashed in the oven." She looked at me. "Do you think it could have been Dillon?"

I thought about the look on Dillon's face when he realized that after everything, the painting wasn't there. I felt angry myself. It was so unfair. It wasn't like Lena and Leo wanted the painting for any other reason than that they loved it. And Dillon wanted it because he loved them.

In a way, I couldn't blame him for wanting to smash things.

"I guess he's probably so ripped at not finding the painting," I said.

"I'm going to get dressed and go meet Mitch and your parents at the rink," said Aunt Bridget, heading out of the room. "You coming?"

I nodded, and even though it was the last thing I

wanted to do, I threw on some clothes. Aunt Bridget and I walked together down the stairs and outside. It was foggy and drizzly, with a little less traffic than usual. We crossed the street and walked through the gates into the park. Usually I felt this zap of energy when I stepped through them, but something felt definitely wrong today, like the ions that Mr. Kim liked telling us about were way more negative than positive and were pressing me down, making it harder to walk.

A crowd had gathered at the rink. Mitch and my parents were there, along with Jack Mack, and Belle Vera.

I stood back, not wanting to see the damage up close.

I sat down on a bench. I felt numb. I stared at the dead grass, at the bare branches of trees carving black lines into the gray sky. Mom came over and sat next to me. She was dressed in her baby blue fleece jacket and hat and black suede gloves. "Well, Willy, with so many people here, everything will be fixed up in no time."

"What's the point?" I asked. "It'll just happen again."

Mom didn't say anything. I turned to her. "Mom, I just want to go home. I don't want to own a park anymore. I don't want to go to a special school. I'll just come home and be a regular kid."

"I'm sorry, Willy," she said. "You can't come home."

I half got up off the bench. "What do you mean?"

"I've gotten used to the quiet. Sorry, Willy. I can't go back to the old way of life."

My mouth dropped open.

Then she smiled and put her black-gloved hand on my knee. "I'm not really being serious, you know. One of the things I've been doing while you've been away is working on getting a sense of humor."

"Oh," I said, feeling a little stupid. "But I bet you do like it."

"I do not!" she said. "But listen, the real reason you can't come home is that Mr. Kim took me aside yesterday and told me you are making incredible progress."

I swallowed hard. "He hasn't said that to me."

Mom nodded. "He says he knows he's been tough on you, but he says he has to be tough, or you won't be able to take care of the park as you get older."

"I don't want to take care of the park anymore," I said.

"He also says," Mom went on, "that when you get smacked down, you just get right back up and try again. And Mr. Zerbe also told me he would like to give you violin lessons. So, you see, you can't come home." She put her arm around me. "I'm really proud of you, Willy, and I know Dad is, too."

Right at that moment Aunt Bridget came and sat down beside me. She was wearing her long patchwork jacket and long, flowing, sort of silky red pants and red wool mittens. Her hair was loose and curling around her rosy cheeks. It made me smile to see how different she looked from my mother.

Aunt Bridget put a red-mittened hand on my knee. "It's going to be all right, Willy. This community rallies in a crisis."

I looked down, but didn't say anything.

"Look, there's Dillon!" she exclaimed.

All the Derondas were approaching, Leo and Lena, Gino, and other uncles I had seen over the weeks working in the park. Dillon was with them. I jumped to my feet, my stomach churning.

Dillon saw me and came right over, his family behind him.

"I didn't do it, Willy," he said, facing me squarely.

"He couldn't have done it," Leo jumped in. He was trembling like an old leaf. "He no do this bad thing. He was with us, all the night, in the hospital. His papa's in a bad way."

Other people were gathering now, Mitch and Belle among them.

"Then who?" someone asked.

"I have a good idea who," said Dillon, his face dark and angry.

"Come on, we help to clean up this mess," said Leo. "We got more bricks somewhere, Gino?"

Gino nodded. "We build again, no problem."

Dillon and I stood together without saying anything for a moment.

"I don't know where the painting is, you know," I said finally.

"I know," he said.

"I'm sorry about the painting, and I'm sorry about your dad," I said.

Dillon seemed to pull into himself. "He's feeling bad about a lot of stuff, and it's making him feel sicker. I keep thinking if I could find the painting . . . But come on, my grandfather's trying to pick up that wheelbarrow. He still thinks he's twenty."

We spent the rest of the day working, replacing boards and logs and bricks, and recementing and scrubbing.

A lot of people arrived throughout the day and helped out, people as old as Leo and as young as Fernando. By nightfall we had made a lot of progress. Mitch was able to fire up the oven, and we pulled benches over and sat on them and relaxed while Lena and Belle and Mitch made pizzas. Zio slid them into the oven on long-handled wooden paddles, and pretty soon the air was filled with that pizza smell you could walk a mile for.

Old Violet approached, pushing her shopping cart filled to the top with plastic bags and a blanket. Zio saw her and waved one of the paddles at her. "Here," he called over to her. "Have some pizza, fresh from the oven."

Old Violet happened to sit down on a bench next to me. She blew on the pizza, cooling it off, and then she sank her dentures into it. I thought of Dennis Quick saying he liked being a dentist so he could help people chew.

The whole day we worked in the park, no one played music in Mr. Pettingill's apartment. But now, suddenly, someone was playing the tuba. It was such a funny, deep, *oompah-pah* sound, it made everyone laugh. And soon we were all chowing down the pizzas and talking and making jokes, and acting as if the whole day had been just one big party.

I didn't want all this to be wrecked again. I went over to Dillon and pulled him aside. "Listen," I said. "They'll let us fix it up, and then they'll attack again."

"Featherstone and Brookings," he said.

I nodded. "We have to come out here every night and keep guard. I'll tell all the Gorillas and the kids I go to school with, and you tell all the Sharks. And we'll bring cameras, like we did on Halloween, and catch them in the act."

"But, hey," said Dillon, "this time you can leave the gorilla suits at home." He smiled weakly.

thirty

I don't need much. A roof over my head,
a bowl of good soup.
—Zio Aguilar

We met at the fountain—Gorillas and Sharks and
Gill Park Gallery School kids. We'd told our families
different things, like I'd told mine I was going to be
out late rehearsing with Dillon and Liesl.

Wildman stepped forward, the collar of his trench
coat pulled up. He was carrying a large pack, and he
had a flashlight strapped to his forehead.

"Here's the map," he said, pulling it out of the
pack. We gathered around it. "There are twenty-one
of us here, twenty-two if you count Ernesto Peligroso," he added quickly, before Fernando could say

anything. "We can have two or three people assigned to each section, but I suggest heavier coverage in southeast B."

"Where the skating rink, rink house, and bake oven are," I said, looking at the map.

"Right," he said. He reached into his pack. "I have two sets of walkie-talkies. One person in each quadrant can carry one, and we can check in with each other."

Dillon and I ended up patrolling one side of the southeast corner together, Gabriela, Gareth, and Liesl taking the other side.

It was dark except for where the streetlamps cast little, lonely, foggy islands of light. And it was quiet. The tuba had stopped its *oompah*-ing. No music played into the park now. The only sound was the occasional honking of a car.

I reached out, feeling the bark of a tree. Even now, in winter, you could feel it was alive, but waiting, like we were waiting, waiting for something to happen. I was glad I was with Dillon. He wouldn't get riled or bothered by anything.

There was plenty to be spooked about walking around the park at night. Things that looked ordinary in the day, like trash cans, seemed threatening, as if globby things would come out of them and grab us. The toolshed, just up ahead, with its utility light on, seemed comforting and solid compared with the dark, shadowy trees.

Suddenly we heard hushed voices, and then we saw the beam of a flashlight and two dark shapes coming our way. Dillon grabbed my arm and pulled me behind the shed. I tensed, clutching the camera I'd bought only an hour ago.

"They look big," I whispered, feeling my heart beginning to race. I wished we had the walkie-talkie to call in others to help us, but Gareth had it.

"Yeah," Dillon whispered back.

"Let's start here." We heard a man's voice, deep and low.

There was a loud sound of glass being shattered, and what light there had been disappeared. The hair on the back of my neck stood up.

For a moment everything was dead quiet again, and then there was the familiar hiss of paint being released from a can. It went on and on.

"What are they doing?" I leaned in close to Dillon's ear.

"They're having a party," he whispered back. "Come on, let's move in. You go around that side. I'll go this way. When you get to the corner, jump out and take the picture. I'll do the same."

Dillon moved away from me, crouching low, quick and quiet as a cat.

"This stuff is making me sick," a man's voice said.

"Don't stop now." Another man's voice rose above the sound of the spray-painting.

Did I recognize those voices? I couldn't be sure.

I started inching around, camera still clutched in my sweaty hand. Contact with the shed wall kept me steady. I came around the first corner and inched along the side. Now I was just coming to the last corner. What if we didn't get to them in time?

I stepped past the edge of the shed, held the camera up, and my finger pressed the button. The camera flashed. On the opposite side, Dillon's flashed, too. We had reached the corners of the shed at the same time.

There was a yell, and then I felt a heavy hand on my shoulders. There were bright beams of light in my eyes now, so bright I couldn't see. Whoever had hold of me started shaking me, hard. The camera dropped out of my hands. And then I was shoved from behind, so I staggered forward, almost knocking into Dillon.

We were surrounded by policemen now, three or four, at least.

"Well, at last. We've caught the famous Blue Gang. I told you they'd be out tonight." I turned toward the familiar voice. The bright beams were no longer shining in my eyes. I could see Frank Featherstone standing just outside the circle of policemen, and next to him was Roland Brookings, Jr.

"And who does it turn out to be?" Frank Featherstone was saying. "The famous Willy Wilson, owner of Gill Park himself. Who would have thought?"

Dillon started lunging at him, fists up. A cop held him back.

The others on our patrol had arrived now—Gareth, Liesl, Gabriela. They looked young and scared, probably the way I looked.

"So what is this? More members of the gang?" Featherstone drawled.

"Don't be ridiculous," Gareth snapped. "Why would Willy Wilson destroy his own park?"

"I can't tell you that, but I *can* tell you he was caught red-handed," Mr. Featherstone said with a sneer. He kicked a can of spray paint so that it rolled toward my feet. I looked down for the camera, but I couldn't see it.

The door to the shed opened, and a large, burly figure stepped out. Someone shone a flashlight full on his face. It was Zio, his eyes dark with anger. "Those kids didn't do nothing," he barked. "I've seen *him* plenty of nights," he said, jerking his head toward Dillon. "But tonight it was *them*." He pointed at Frank Featherstone and Roland Brookings.

"What?" A buzz of voices grew loud and angry.

Zio raised his voice. "Soon as I heard the light get smashed, I cracked open the door, took a look, and what do you know, two grown men with cans of spray paint in their hands, acting like a pair of loopy kids."

"You expect anyone to believe that?" Featherstone laughed a short, barky laugh, but I thought Brookings looked nervous. He hadn't said a word, either, not the whole time we had been standing there.

"You're telling us you just happened to be in that toolshed?" one of the policemen said, sounding as if he'd been told a joke that he didn't really get.

"That's right," said Zio.

"At this time of night? What were you doing in there?" the same policeman asked.

"I was having myself some soup."

"What?"

"It's my home," Zio said. "Old Violet fixed it up nice for me." He turned back to the door and opened it wider. We all stepped forward, crowding in to see. There was a bare lightbulb hanging from the ceiling, a chair and a mattress on the floor, a little table, and a hot plate with a saucepan on it. The smell of soup wafted out.

And on the wall was a painting.

I looked around for Dillon. He was right next to me, and he saw it just a split second after I did. He whooped, and almost sprang straight into the air.

"Where'd you get that painting?" I crushed forward, trying to get to Zio.

He looked at me and blinked. "I . . . I was just . . . I borrowed it," he said.

"BORROWED it?" Dillon yelled.

"It . . . it was for my house. I just wanted a painting of my own, on my own wall, for a short time."

"Come on, let's move along now." A policeman grabbed me by the arm and started pulling me along.

"The cameras," Dillon muttered. "We have to find the cameras." He bent down on his hands and knees, scrabbling in the leaves until a policeman grabbed him and jerked him to his feet. I tried feeling the ground with my feet, desperately trying to find mine before I was pulled away. I couldn't find it. I looked for one of the cans of spray paint. They could at least try testing it for fingerprints, but they seemed to have disappeared, too.

Along with Featherstone and Brookings.

I realized with a shock as we were being herded out of the park that those two clowns were nowhere to be seen.

thirty-one

When a play goes well, you feel like you've
been shot out of a cannon and landed
in a field of flowers.
—Jack Mack

My father and Gareth's father both came down to
the police station. Zio described again what he had
seen. No one really knew if they could believe him,
and they weren't sure they could believe us, either.
In the end, to make everyone feel better, the police
decided that every kid who was in the park that
night should do community service.

And Zio returned the painting to Dillon's family.
No one—not Merla, not Leo or Lena—wanted to press
charges.

We spent the whole weekend working. On Saturday we scrubbed the stuff off Zio's toolshed. We put a new coat of paint on all the benches and lampposts. We raked leaves and mulched Mitch's garden. We set up half a dozen bike racks and replaced the trash baskets.

On Saturday night we had a rehearsal for the play. Our first performance was going to be at the end of the next week, on Friday, and Jack was getting intense.

Even though most of us were tired from working in the park all day, Jack drove us hard. He kept stopping us. And stopping us. And stopping us. I thought we were all going to kill him before the night was over. He was trying to fix every little thing, and then at the end he made us sit there for his "notes," his feedback on what we were doing right—but mostly wrong.

On Sunday, Mitch brought in a couple of cords of wood, and we split logs for the rink-house fireplace and the bake oven. Belle bought dishes and silverware and pots and pans from the Salvation Army, and we washed them and then stacked them in the rink-house kitchen. It was unusually warm, and the ground was still soft, so we planted hundreds of flower bulbs all over the park.

Aunt Bridget came out and helped us. She kept shaking her head as she gazed over at the new Featherstone buildings. "Sometimes new buildings look like fake teeth," she said. "They're too big, and they look out of place."

Sunday night's rehearsal was mostly chaos. It was a full-dress rehearsal. All along, Aunt Bridget had been trying costumes out on us, but this was the first time we wore all the masks, the headpieces, everything. This was the first time Liesl swung out on the rope in her monkey outfit. She did fine, hanging by one arm and swinging her long tail with the other.

On Monday poor Zio was so embarrassed and ashamed he started crying when he saw us at the Gallery School. He stood on the landing, holding his hat in his hands, talking to us as we came up the stairs. "I liked how Saint Francis was talking to the birds," he said sadly. "It's what I do in the park sometimes—talk to the birds. They are the only ones I can talk to sometimes who don't think I'm crazy. I didn't think of it as stealing," he went on. "I was just borrowing it. Just for the time Merla was gone. I didn't think she'd miss it when she wasn't even there."

It was horrible, watching the tears spill out of his dark eyes. Liesl stalked off, her face stiff, her hands balled into fists.

"How can I be a guard in an art gallery? A guard who steals paintings! Itsuko should fire me, but she won't."

Itsuko happened to walk up the stairs just as he was saying this. "You're a guard who loves paintings, that's what you are," she said. Her eyes were brown today, maybe her real color, and they looked soft and warm and not mad at all. "And we couldn't manage without you."

I was surprised by how right it seemed to be sitting down at the long table and starting up school again. I could finally look at Mr. Kim without feeling a lurch in the pit of my stomach. "Welcome back," he said. "Let's talk about the paper you handed in before Thanksgiving, Willy." He placed it on the table in front of me. I glanced at it out of the corner of my eye, automatically checking it for red marks. It seemed pretty clear, like a leg that has come through sliding into second base without getting too many scrapes. "We don't give grades here at the Gill Park Gallery School, but if we did, do you know what this paper would receive?"

I shook my head, afraid of hearing the answer.

"What, do you suppose, is the first letter of the alphabet?"

We all groaned.

Mr. Kim pushed at the middle of his glasses and smiled, so that his eyes turned into two straight lines. "The letter *A* started out as an Egyptian hieroglyph representing the head of an ox; turned into the Hebrew word *aleph,* meaning "ox"; and then became the Greek letter *alpha.*"

That night, rehearsal was long and hard again. Jack had convinced Zio to run the lights because he was smart and quick about stuff like that, but this was the first time we'd run through the play with them. We also went through the scenery changes, which we had to make happen ourselves.

And then finally, on Tuesday, Jack ran the play

without stopping us once. The villagers danced; the drummers drummed; we came out in our costumes; and if someone dropped a line, we just kept going anyway.

At the end of the rehearsal, the houselights went on, and we sat down to wait for Jack's notes.

Jack stood in front of us. After three nights of nagging, we didn't know what to expect. He rubbed his shiny bald head, stared at us for a moment without any expression on his face, and then he held his arms straight up in the air. "Hallelujah, we have a play!" he shouted, a huge smile on his face. He grabbed Aunt Bridget and swung her around. "We have a play!" He let go of Aunt Bridget and pointed to us. "You did it! You guys did it! And Kizzi!" He pulled Kizzi up out of her chair. "Kizzi, I could *hear* you, you darling, adorable girl!"

We rehearsed one more time on Wednesday night, and it felt even smoother and better than the night before. Since we finally knew what we were doing, we started having fun. It was hard to believe that only a few days ago I had been sure the play was going to be a total flop. Now I couldn't wait for the performance.

Jack didn't ask us to come in at all on Thursday. He told us to rest up and go over our lines. And then on Friday we opened. My parents came, and Mitch and Belle, a dozen Derondas, and everyone else's families, too, plus lots of people who weren't even related to us, like Itsuko and Hans Zerbe, as well as others we didn't know but who had read about the play in the paper. The theater was packed, and Jack's grin was as wide as a mile. He hadn't been sure anyone would come, although Aunt Bridget kept saying, "Of course they will."

At first, I was so nervous I didn't feel as if I'd be able to walk out onstage, but gradually, I could feel all those people out there in the audience becoming my friends. They *liked* me. They laughed in the right places. They even clapped in the part where Dillon and Liesl and I all landed on top of each other.

"I can't believe you were able to memorize all those lines," my mother kept saying when it was over.

And then Leo and Lena came up to me. "Tomorrow, you come to our home and we celebrate," Lena said.

"For the return of our *tesoro*," Leo said with shining eyes. "And for the friendship you have made with our boy."

On Saturday afternoon I started out for the South Park, heading in the direction of the new Featherstone buildings. I flashed on Featherstone and Brookings sneaking around in the park. I couldn't believe they'd gotten away with pinning the vandalism on us. It still made me mad to think about it.

As I rode up Smart Street, I also couldn't help thinking of Dillon's dad, and I wondered how he was doing.

Dillon greeted me at the door. "Hey," he said. His upper lip twitched. I think he was feeling just as happy to see me as I was to see him, but you couldn't ever really tell with Dillon.

"Come on," he said. "My grandparents are waiting to see you."

As I came into the kitchen I noticed right away the little painting hanging on its place on the wall. I went up close to it.

"Go ahead," said Leo. "You can touch it. It has stayed good for seven hundred year—it will last a little longer."

I ran my finger lightly on Saint Francis's brown robe. It was amazing to think that the man who had painted this had lived during the time that Saint Francis had walked around barefoot, giving money to the poor and talking to the animals.

Both Lena and Leo gave me a big hug, and then telling me to sit down, they started bustling around, fussing over refreshments. Dillon sat at the table across from me.

"The lady at the gallery, she offer us much money for the painting," said Lena, "and we think maybe we sell so Dillon can go to a good college."

"But he say no," said Leo proudly. "He say his pitching arm take him wherever he want to go, and the painting, she stay with us."

He sat down next to Dillon and put his arm around him. Dillon patted the old man back.

"And Dino," Leo went on, "he much, much better."

"He maybe come to live with us after he come out of the hospital," said Lena, pouring out fresh lemonade for us all. "He live here, and see Santo Francesco every day. Our *tesoro*, it will inspire him, no?" She put the pitcher down and stood with her hands on her hips staring at the painting. "I know why that man Zio take the painting. He mean no harm. I am sorry he has no painting of his own now."

"Yeah, too bad," Dillon muttered. "I feel real sorry for him."

Leo gave him a light swat on the side of his head. "He got a ways to go, this boy," he said, turning to me. "Is making progress, but Roma, she wasn't built in a night."

thirty-two

Responsibility's like this new jacket you
have to put on. It feels stiff and heavy, and
you can't move your arms. But after a while
you start getting used to it, and if someone
asked you to take it off, you wouldn't.
—*Willy Wilson*

The next day, Sunday, we had a matinee show early
enough so that it was still light out by the time we
had finished, scrubbed off the makeup, and put the
costumes away.

"Hey," said Gareth as we stepped out of the Art
Factory. "Let's go hit a few."

The thought of baseball seemed to pull us all like a magnet. Gareth stopped by his house and picked up some bats and balls and gloves, and then there we all were, most of the kids from the show, running for the park. It felt so good to be outside in the fresh air after being under the hot stage lights for two hours.

On the way over to the field, we saw Mitch and Zio and some of the Derondas hard at work building something.

"It's a guardhouse," Mitch said, looking up as we stopped for a moment to watch. "The park needs a guard, Zio needs a house, and so . . ."

Zio didn't say anything, but a big smile crept across his face.

And then there we were, out on the field, hitting some, throwing some. Before long, Toenail showed up, and Hoscowitz, Capasso, Dixon—the Gorilla regulars. I looked around for Liesl. She had been with us when we left the theater, but she wasn't here now. And then the Sharks began showing up.

"Okay," said Dillon. "Time for a game. Who's up first?"

Gareth tossed a coin into the air. "Heads it's Gorillas, tails it's Sharks."

The Gorillas were up, Capasso first at bat. I sat on the bench waiting my turn. Zack appeared, playing his harmonica.

"Oh, Zack! Who're ya gonna play for?" We gave him a hard time. "Come on, Zackie, you gotta make up your mind."

Zack stood there, still playing his harmonica, looking first at the Sharks out on the field and then at us, the Gorillas, sitting on the bench. "Hmm," he was saying when Gabriela and Fernando showed up.

"Hi, guys," said Gabriela in that spicy way of hers.

"We're busy right now, Gabriela," said Dillon. "Get a glove if you want to play. Otherwise, get off the field."

Gabriela put her hands on her hips and looked at Dillon for a moment. Then she turned to me. "I got something to show you."

"Not right now," said Dillon.

Gabriela marched right up to him and grabbed him by the arm and yanked him over to me. "Someday you're going to learn when it's time to listen," she said to him. "Look at what I got." She handed me an envelope.

I opened it and pulled out a photograph. It was a little blurry, but not so bad that you couldn't tell exactly what was going on. There was the toolshed with the smashed utility light, where Zio had lived for a couple of months without anyone knowing. There was all the blue that was being spray-painted on the wall. And there were two men holding cans of spray paint, and they were easy to recognize.

"Wow," was all Dillon and I could say.

"I went back and looked for those cameras again," said Gabriela. "I think Featherstone must have nabbed one of them. I saw him messing about on his hands and knees in the leaves while the cops were talking to you. But I found the other one a few feet away. And it came out real good, didn't it?"

"Yeah," I said. "Real good."

Gabriela grinned. "And so now the newspaper gets a little present from an anonymous source."

"Wow," I said again. I looked out toward the South Park, feeling lighter than I had in weeks. Featherstone didn't get to have everything he wanted, after all. And Brookings, he wasn't going to get his hands on my park—no sir, not ever. And maybe after this he'd stop trying.

Dillon suddenly threw his arms around Gabriela and lifted her off the ground and swung her around. "Whoee!" he shouted. "You are one great dame!"

"All right, I want to play now," said Gabriela, laughing, her face bright red as he put her down.

"You play on *my* team," Dillon said.

"Ernesto Peligroso and I want to play, too," Fernando said, coming over and hanging on Dillon's arm.

"Okay, you'll be lucky for us," said Dillon.

All this time Wildman had been standing on the sidelines, watching. We'd forgotten about him and unbelievably, he hadn't butted in and put himself on a team. Dillon nodded his chin slightly toward him. "Okay, buddy, we need you. Come on."

Wildman flung his arms up in the air. *"Yes!"* he yelled out, and sort of lumbered onto the field like a big bear. "I warn you, I'm a total klutz, but I'm good at strategy."

"Yeah," said Dillon. "Strategy is good." He wound up for the pitch, stuck his leg back, cocked his head sideways a few times. It occurred to me he looked a lot like he was doing one of the crazy bird dances the villagers did in the play.

I ran over to the bench to sit down and wait for my turn to be up to bat. Liesl slipped onto the bench and sat right beside me.

"Where ya been?" I asked.

"Finishing up something for Zio," she said mysteriously. I looked at her hands. Her long fingers were covered with paint. "Thought he needed something to hang on his new wall," she said.

I turned sideways to look at her. "You painted him a painting," I said.

She shrugged her bony little shoulders. "I hated seeing him cry like that," she said.

"What did you paint him?" I asked.

"Old Violet sitting on her bench yelling at the birds," she said.

I could just picture it, and it made me laugh. "Maybe it will stay in his family for seven hundred years," I said.

"Hey, Wilson!" Gareth was shouting. "You're up."

Giving the bat a few practice swings, I walked over to the plate. Way across the park, over the tops of the trees, I caught sight of the deck of a house. I was pretty sure I could just make out a glint of light. Maybe Hans Zerbe was outside watching us through his telescope today.

From Mr. P.'s apartment piano music played, the

left hand keeping rhythm like the regular beating of my heart, the right hand dancing out a jazzy tune.

"Hey, Willy, this ain't no time for daydreamin'!"

I looked at Dillon, who was calling out to me with a big grin on his face. He hadn't called me Shark Bait—he'd actually used my name. Two months ago, he'd been my enemy. I planted my feet and faced him squarely.

He'd always be a Shark, and I'd always be a Gorilla, but I figured in the big picture he and I were on the same team.